HIS HIDDEN TREASURES

HIS HIDDEN TREASURES

CONTAINED WITHIN YOUR CIRCUMSTANCES

CHERYL STASINOWSKY

WORD SCRIBE

I dedicate this book to my children, their children,
and to the generations that I will never have an
opportunity to personally speak to.
I am writing this book with you in my heart.
I hand you my private processing of my faith and I bless you
on your own personal journey of faith with your Lord Jesus Christ.
I love you and am praying for you right now, as I am alive.

How awesome is that!

My Family

Contents

Acknowledgements

Father, Son, and the Holy Spirit

You are truly the Author and Finisher of my faith. Thank You for allowing me to co-author this book with You. Thank You for teaching me to pay attention to what is really happening within me. I love processing life with You. I absolutely love each of You individually and as a whole. Thank You!

My Mom and Dad

I thank you for bringing me into the world and for taking care of me and providing for me. Thank you for what you have taught me and contributed to who I am today. I love you both.

My Husband

Wow, you are truly an amazing man, husband and father. I love you. You have believed in me when I did not believe in myself. Thank you for enduring, loving, caring and providing through all for me and our children. My thank you will never be big enough or compare to how you have held true to our vows of for better or for worse, for richer or for poorer, in sickness and in health and we will be together until death do us part. Thank you for my morning coffees. Many times we have been the iron that sharpens iron. I love you.

My Children, Amber and Jordan

I am continually amazed and in awe of who you are both becoming.
You are both a cherished gift from God. I have learned much from
both of you and you are contained within the pages of this book.
My heart and prayer for your life is that you will find Jesus in all
that you encounter every day. Thank you for loving me. I love you
both so much!

My Friends and Family

In whatever capacity our paths of life have crossed, I thank you.
I thank you for your prayers, your listening ears, your words
spoken to me and your encouragement. May you be eternally and
abundantly blessed all the days of your life.

Note from Author

The intent of this book is not for the reader to sit and read from cover to cover, but to read a chapter as a devotional, then allow the Holy Spirit to reveal the truth and work within you.

The writings of this book took place over a two year period of my life. At this point, the Lord asked my husband and I to shut down our 18 year business, sell nearly everything (including our dream house), and move across the United States to go to ministry school. After our first year of ministry school, the Lord positioned us in New Zealand, where we journeyed for four months and moved 12 times. From here He moved us to Australia for 14 months, and we soon realized God had put us there to bring additional breaking and striping in our lives. Upon our return from this intense time, we encountered yet additional workings on our hearts, souls, minds, and emotions. It is in that time period after getting back to the States that these writings were produced.

Introduction

"Again, the kingdom of heaven is like treasure hidden in a field, which a man found and hid; and for joy over it he goes and sells all that he has and buys that field" (Matthew 13:44).

Contained within the pages of this book you will find parts of me and of my journey to uncover the hidden treasures the Lord has placed in my life.

Each section tells of a victory experienced when I found what was hidden in the struggles, the pain, the offenses, the relationships and the behaviors that have exposed in me what is not of Him. I have experienced great healing from the touch of the Holy Spirit and have learned to look for the good in each situation and find God in it. No matter what we encounter, He is there.

I guarantee that if you read this book and allow the Lord to work in you through it, you will not be the same as you are right now. There is testimony contained within these pages for you. I believe that within the words of these pages are keys to bring freedom to the Body of Christ. How do I know this? I am living proof; I have experienced the working of His hand and of His Word in my life, through all. I am telling you that there are hidden treasures for you in this book. Enjoy the search, and thank Jesus for all you receive.

I pray that you will find yourself within the pages of my journey and that there will be favorites you will read over and over again. You may also find resistance rise up within you as you read certain ones; embrace it and do not reject it, for it is the work of the Holy Spirit. He is always working on our behalf.

"If you seek her as silver, and search for her as for hidden treasures; then you will understand the fear of the LORD, and find the knowledge of God" (Proverbs 2:4-5).

MY HEART AND BETRAYAL

When we arrived home in America from Australia, we walked into an enormous mess. We were very tired and had so much to unpack and get used to again. We had been away from our home in South Carolina for nearly eighteen months. Our home, rental properties and finances were not in the condition that we had expected or hoped for. I am being very careful not to blame or judge, as really the situation we encountered was a situation the Lord used to expose deeper hurts of the past. To give some background, we came home to four empty rental properties, much garbage and trash everywhere, dirty properties that had to be cleaned, items missing within our home, no jobs, no hope of much of a future (we had just finished two years of ministry school and the expectation that some ministry would come knocking on our door to employ us, did not happen). We were tired, our money was running low, we had boxes to unpack and not many friends, because many of the people we knew had moved on. It was unbelievably hard.

I struggled internally and deeply with feeling betrayed, lied to, stolen from, as the renters did not pay their rent, made promises, and then disappeared. I could not seem to let it go; even though I wanted to and knew I needed to, I could not. There was something within me that wanted revenge. It was ugly. One of the people who was, at the time, the main source of most the grief, just disappeared and left all the trash for us to clean up. I kept thinking that I wanted it resolved. *Lord, we need to get this resolved, but he will not come out of hiding.* For days, I struggled with how in the world to let it go and not just bury it. So, one day I sat down and asked the Lord to show me what was going on within my heart. It could not really be about the situation. I needed freedom, and so I waited to get the answers. *Lord, what is going on in me?* Here is a summary of what He showed me: You do not want resolution; you want to blame and point fingers and make him feel as bad as you do. You are disguising revenge with the word *resolution.* He was right. *So, how in the world do I get free of this?* I forgave and repented, and then the Lord allowed me to see that He understood betrayal, and asked me to look at His betrayer and what He walked through. My situation did not seem so bad. I felt the freedom as I let it go and the anger was gone. I got to experience one of the sufferings of Jesus. I cannot tell you I was totally jumping for joy that I got to experience this, but I understood and thanked Him.

I thought I was finished with it, until the father of the person wanted to come and get his son's stuff, and something again rose up inside of me. I have learned to pay attention to what is going on within me. The following morning, the Lord woke me up and asked me if I wanted to know the root of what was going on within me, I said that I did. He starting showing me years of situations in which I have felt the very same way I do now. He showed me times in my life when I cleaned up or took care of a mess that I felt was not mine to deal with and I felt that I got stuck with it. I repented and forgave. As I lay there, I said, *Lord, all I know to do is repent and forgive them.* I do not know how to bring the healing and freedom that I need here. So, I waited. Then, He showed me many situations in which clients in our business had not paid us, and had lied to us, and promised things and did not come through. I repented and forgave. Then, He showed me employees who we had helped and what they did to us. I repented and forgave. Then, He showed me how people in leadership positions had made promises of helping and did not follow through. I repented and forgave. Then, He showed me our rental properties and how we had helped the renters and believed and trusted in them and they did not pay; they left in the middle of the night after not paying rent for four months, and trashed the place as well, and they lied and stole from us. I repented and forgave. Then, I waited and thanked the Lord for showing me the years of betrayal that were within me, and He used this one situation, which was pretty extreme, to get my attention and show me what was buried within my heart.

I have come to realize that the fire and hand of God upon our lives can be painful, and that we have a choice to sit with our Father and ask Him what in the world is going on within us, or to blame the other person and take no personal responsibility for it. Our trials serve to expose our heart and the unresolved issues of our past that we think are over and done with.

I wrote this in my journal: *Oh Lord, I love You. I love You, Holy Spirit, alive within me. I feel Your stirring and Your anointing and I love it. It is so very encouraging. A drink of fresh water to a dry and thirsty soul. I am encouraged that newness is awakening within me. Like after the winter and green pushes forth new life, as leaves appear on trees, grass greens, flowers come forth. Oh Lord, like after a big forest fire and all is dead and lifeless, and then a rain comes, and eventually life returns and the forest is alive again. I, too, am feeling the new life moving within me. So good, Lord. I so have yearned and wondered if that wonderful, peaceful stirring would again be a part of my life. My soul is just smiling!*

I am not through all of this yet, but as I look over the ashes of the fire that has been burning up the chaff in my life, I see hope of little green sprouts starting to come up through the black of the ashes. Yes, these are the hidden treasures that we receive when we wait upon the Lord and ask Him to expose the deepest places within our hearts. He knows them and He knows what to do to help us. I cannot say that what He does feels like it is help in any way, shape or form while I am in the middle of it. But as my head is poking up through the ashes and the light of God is shining on me, I have deep hope in God. May the testimony of this word bring freedom to others. Please remember this is my journey and I am always a work in progress, but grab onto the hope that is within these words to get you through your own situations.

WASH OVER ME, OH LORD

I have not written like this for a very long time, but this morning I went somewhere with the Lord and I want to take you there with me. My spirit is excited with the thought of doing this, so I am going to take a risk and invite you, in the Spirit, to join me. The Spirit of the living God, who is within you, knows this place very well, so I want to encourage you, not to just not think about it, but read with your heart and allow the Lord to show you where we are going.

I am walking on this path in the middle of the most lush green plants in an almost forest-like setting. It is so peaceful and quiet. As I am walking on this path, I am drawn to the sound of rain. I am almost running at the anticipation of what is coming. It starts to rain ever so gently, and it is refreshing. It is not cold, nor do I care in the least that I am getting wet. I keep walking. It starts raining more intensely, and finally, I am standing under a waterfall. Oh, the refreshment of the cleansing is like standing under a hot shower on a cold day. Your body just relaxes at the warmth. I want to stand under this waterfall and let the water saturate every part of my being. Oh, such a place of pure peace where nothing else matters. All that is within me wants to rejoice that I am alive. I want to praise the Lord for everything in my life, bad and good. I am so filled to overflowing with the presence of God that time stands still. In His presence truly is fullness of joy. Come and drink with me as I am there once again. Let us just praise Him:

Oh Lord, You are more than enough for me. I love You. I love Your presence. I love everything about You. More, Lord; please fill me with more of You. When I am weak, You are strong. When I am not faithful, You are always faithful. I am not impossible for You. There is nothing that You cannot do. You are my All in All and beyond. Oh God, let Your glory fill the earth today. Thank You for this day that I am breathing and living, and have another day to let You walk on this earth through me. There is nothing that compares with You. Breathe through every pore of my body and touch others through me today. Oh, You are amazing. You are beautiful beyond description. Thank You for this time of refreshment right now when the cares of this world have been put aside and nothing matters but this time with You. Continue to take me, and the others who have joined us today, to this secret place. Oh, Your peace that passes understanding is what I live for every moment. You are the calm in the storms of my life. You are the solid Rock on which I stand and will cling to. You will see me through. You know the way and I am staying with You. Thank You for carrying me and loving me even when I am fighting You in my flesh. I say to my flesh, you must die so that You may live within me in greater fullness. Uncover the places of my heart that are hardened against You and surround them with Your gentle, healing love. Oh, all of my fears, Lord, please take them into Your love as well, and may they all be cast away, because Your perfect love casts out all fear. Bless You, Lord. May You be abundantly and exceedingly blessed today with me. May my life today bless You beyond all, not because of what I do or say, but because my heart is reaching out and saying yes, Lord. All that is within me is opening up to Your plans and purposes for my life today. May my every breath, and each step I take in faith today, compel You to be proud of me. You are the way, the truth and the life. All of You completely in all of me. Overwhelm me with You, and may we be as one today. I am in absolute love with You. Teach me more and more about You and Your love. Amen!

I pray that it was a wonderful time with the Lord for you as it was for me. When I went to this place the first time, His living water uncovered areas of my heart that were covered and caked in dirt. I did not even know they were there, because they had been buried. But what I want to share is that as His living water washed over these areas, I felt no shame or condemnation. I allowed Him to show me the areas; I easily repented and asked Him to change my mindsets about these things. I submitted to His touch, and it was so gentle. I felt no resistance rise up, because I felt safe with Him. He took me to a place where I was secure and not afraid. I did not pretend to be something that I am not. He knows who I am better than I do. So, this living water cleansed me and washed over me and opened up an area of my heart to love Him more.

If you have walked through a similar thing while reading this today, open your heart, mind and spirit to the gentle touch of His hand to remove the areas of your past that are hindering a deeper and more openly loving relationship with Him, the keeper of your heart and the lover of your soul.

The other day, I was going to go for a walk and our puppy wanted to go. But lately when I have taken him he has been running off, so today he needed to be on a leash for the first time. He resisted and fought and turned and refused to walk with that leash on. I kept pulling and encouraging him, as I knew he would get to go and do what he loved to do if he would submit to the leash. The leash was for his safety, but he did not see it that way. Eventually, he stopped resisting and I praised him, and then we went for our walk. He loved it. The next day, when it was time to go for a walk again, I pulled out the leash and put it on him fairly easily and we went, no resistance. This was such a good illustration of how the Lord is with us. He knows what is best for us and we resist it and fight it and even try to run the other way. We even, at times, can cause ourselves much pain, like my puppy inflicted on himself as he pulled away. But the Lord is sure in what He is doing, and He knows what is coming, just as I knew that Blessing (our puppy) was going to really enjoy the walk that was coming. The trials and tribulations are just preparing us for something else that is coming. We can resist or we can submit and trust that He knows what He is doing.

I want to encourage you to go away daily with the Lord and allow Him to search your heart, and then submit to His touch on the areas He is exposing. Allow Him to use even this writing to take you to that place of safety with Him. I could stay there all day and just enjoy Him. My prayer and purpose for even writing this is to allow you to see His hand and take it and go with Him. I have to share Him with you. My heart just wants everyone to be with Him through everything. Enjoy Him today!

ALL CREATION
WORSHIPS HIM

I was driving in my car listening to worship music when I had a moment of revelation. As I was listening, I could feel the person singing the song the Lord put inside of them to sing. I could sense that all of creation around me had a song of worship to their Creator. I felt in the Spirit everything poised to worship.

As I began really looking at what He was showing me, I noticed just about everything I looked at in nature grew in an upward direction. Gravity pulls us all downward, and yet, creation defies gravity, in a sense, by growing up. As I looked at the trees and plants and flowers, I could see that they look toward heaven. It is as if they are showing off the glory of the Lord. I just kept looking and looking and was in awe.

Even when it is wintertime and cold, the plants grow up to heaven. With no leaves, broken, half dead, and the rain pouring down, they praise the Lord. Look at the trees around you. Can you see them in worship? With our hands lifted to heaven and our arms open wide, are we not resembling nature in worship of our Creator?

We can learn from the nature that He has surrounded us with. It has no fear of man; it worships anyway. It does not care if we are looking at it; nature worships night and day, 24/7, 365 days a year. If that piece of God's creation falls over, part of it is still reaching up to heaven in worship. Green or brown, flowers or not, it is worshiping the Creator. Are we? Is the very nature around us, an example left for us to follow? Did our Father put it there just for us to eat the fruit, smell the flowers and enjoy the colors, or is there still another aspect of nature that we can learn from?

Have you ever had something inside of you that just had to get out, in a good way? I mean, you are just so filled with the joy and excitement of the Lord that you tell everyone you meet about it. Has gravity held you down? I see gravity as the enemy, (in a way). His gravity would be discouragement, depression, hopelessness, fear of man, fearfulness, worry, and all the other cares of this world that keep us looking down instead of up. Nature contends with the same gravity, and yet, continues praising the Creator and giving glory to God. Can you see it?

I heard the singer singing from within. It was just a normal worship song I have heard hundreds of times on the radio, and yet, this morning I felt the Spirit of the living God singing from within, and the singer had to sing. There are different styles, different beats, and it can be loud or soft, but I want to encourage you today to hear what is coming from within. What has the Lord put within you? It does not really even have to be Christian music, as His creation is singing something. I know that lots of the non- Christian music is worshiping the wrong thing, but who put the musical ability within them? Music has been placed within all of us to pour out to someone. Can you see the pouring out?

I am joining with nature today and worshiping through all the trials and tribulations of my day. I am going to be like the trees that have fallen over, and the parts of me that can worship will.

Spirit of the living God, fall fresh on us today and let us join with Your creation in worshiping You. Just as the twenty-four elders are worshiping You night and day continuously, You have also desired that all the earth join with heaven. Oh, may the rocks not have to cry out for lack of our worship of You upon this earth. Help us, mighty, faithful One, to lift all that we are to You and worship in whatever sound, position, or way that we can. May we all find the song You have placed within us to give back to You. May we dance and enjoy You through our day. May our worship join with nature and magnify Your holy name today. We love You and ask for You to open the eyes of our understanding to what nature is singing. More, Lord, more! Yes and amen!

I am learning to praise Him through all. It shifts my focus from me and my current situation to the faithfulness of my Lord and Savior Jesus Christ. His Scripture comes alive within me. My God shall supply all my need according to His riches in glory by Christ Jesus. Not according to my riches, but His. If I stay focused on my riches, (bank accounts, home, talents and gifts, job or lack thereof, etc.) then this opens a door for worry, despair and concern. But when I declare His goodness and faithfulness over my days and situations, the burden lifts and my spirit is not so heavy and I can praise Him more. I am learning to praise Him through all; we can face every situation with Him. I am learning to find His goodness through what I see nature doing. Nature worships in spite of the predators constantly attacking it. May we be as the nature around us and praise and trust the Lord through the storms.

Please be encouraged today. I pray that you will literally hear and see creation praising their Creator today, and that your heart, soul, mind and strength will step into the worship session going on all around you. *Bless You, Lord!*

THE SECRET OF LIVING

I want to really clear away a pile of ashes on something I am just now realizing I am learning. I am not going to deny in any way, shape or form that our time out of the country was a big challenge. I found myself, most days, hoping and praying for the Lord to give me a day of rest. *I need some relief, Lord. I know that You will not give me more than I can handle, but You cannot push me much more or I am going to break.* I longed for the day we would finally get to go back to America and be in our own home again. There is nothing like your own bed and your own space. We even received a word in Australia that we would receive three months of rest before being sent out again. I was really looking forward to some rest from the trials and tribulations I had been enduring the last three and a half years, but which were intensified substantially over the last year and a half.

We got home and immediately encountered issue after issue. I was so tired, so tired of fighting the enemy, so tired of trying to stay focused on what the Lord was doing, so tired of problems and misunderstandings. I wanted to rest, but that was not possible. We had to hit the ground running. I had to really fight in order not to be offended at the Lord for not taking care of things here at home while we were away serving Him in another country. I think you get the picture. I wanted the cruise ship for a while, and I wanted a leave of absence from the battleship.

I have pondered over and over Philippians 4 where Paul writes about rejoicing in the Lord always and then repeats it, in case we forget in a matter of seconds that he already said that. We are to bring our requests before the Lord in prayer and thanksgiving, and then we will have the peace of God rule in our hearts (I am paraphrasing what it means to me.) In the Living Translation, it says in verses 4-5, "Always be full of joy in the Lord. I say it again—rejoice! Let everyone see that you are considerate in all you do." Then continuing down to portions from verses 8-12, "And now,…one final thing. Fix your thoughts on what is true, and honorable, and right, and pure, and lovely, and admirable. Keep putting into practice all you learned… Then the God of peace will be with you. I know how to live on almost nothing or with everything. I have learned the secret of living in every situation."

Paul had learned it. He learned what he wrote about before he wrote about it. I see that verses 4-19 are what he lived. How did he learn to live like that? He had to have the situations and circumstances that came into his life to provide him the training ground for him to learn it. This is the journey all of us are on, the secret of living in every situation, of knowing and walking in complete trust and faith that we can do all things through Christ who strengthens us. We can learn the secret of knowing that our God will supply all our need according to His riches in glory, not our riches, and the secret of knowing that we are more than conquerors through Christ Jesus.

Here is what I am learning. The world around us is filled with trials and tribulations from the enemy, so why do we believe we should have a different life? I had a mindset that since I was a Christian, I would have this easy life (cruise ship). I have to get over that. The thing that makes Jesus so appealing to the unbelievers around us is our response, our journey through the very same trials and tribulations they are encountering. They see us going through financial hardships, deaths, divorces, drug abuse, betrayals, back stabbings and everything else the enemy throws at us. But Philippians 4 is the difference in our lives that causes them to turn their heads and hearts to Jesus. They watch us and then finally get up the desperate courage to ask us how in the world we have peace with everything going wrong around us. Jesus got their attention.

Have we, as Christians, portrayed to others a life of no problems? Have we pretended when we should not have? Just thought I would throw out some interesting questions. How do non-Christians come up with the line "You think you are so perfect?" Do we really think we are fooling them into thinking that? When it gets tough, the real stuff comes out and they see it. What are they seeing in us?

I am learning to focus one day at a time and commit every second to the Lord. I proclaim His goodness daily over my life. I am asking the Lord to help me each day to love my husband and children the way that they need today. I am letting Him direct my path and move my heart to do what He wants me to do. I am not focusing on all the things that need to be done, but only on what He has planned for me today.

I have really had to face this, as a really big hope and desire of mine was to be in full-time ministry. That is the reason I thought I was going to ministry school. I thought I was going to teach and preach the Word of God to thousands. When we came home to a mess, needing jobs, and finding no open doors to a ministry, I had to face that. The Lord gave us a vision to start a business. I never thought I would go into business again. Yes, I seem to have a gifting for it, but I had laid that down to be in full-time ministry. I did not see the business world as a ministry. I am still fighting that. He actually has given me several open doors to businesses, and so I am walking in the direction He is showing.

I have learned that I am in full-time ministry. Ministry is being Jesus to the world around me, going into the homes of non-believers and giving Jesus an opportunity to be in their living rooms for an hour.

He is changing mindsets, and I am using the gifts and talents that He has given me in the marketplace. I can model living and operating a business based on truth and integrity. I can just be Jesus to the ones who really need Him, the ones who are not inside the doors of the church. The ones out there struggling on their own battleships of life trying to find their way through, and searching for any way they can find to relieve the pain. Oh, I understand the pain. I understand the struggles. I understand the daily pressure of paying the bills. I understand and have the answer. I get to bring Jesus, the Answer, into their homes.

I have been paying attention to how often I ask the Lord for a break, and I am turning it around to thank Him for yet another opportunity to learn more about the secret of living for Him. He is not punishing us with the hardships. The hardships are a training ground and a model for the world around us. We have the answer they need. Are we shining His light for the world around us to see? I am trying. Can we really learn to embrace the tests of this life? Tests are not punishment; they are opportunities for us to show the Lord what we have learned, and allow the Lord to show us what is really inside of us. Yes, they are, at times, very painful, I understand. Yes, they are, at times, intensely hard, I understand. We squirm, complain, fight, cry, and wonder why. I am choosing today to learn the secret of living in every situation and rejoicing with all that is within me for the opportunities that help me to learn. Grab the power in this testimony for yourself and walk in a new mindset through your circumstances this day with the Lord.

In case you are finding yourself saying, "You do not understand, my situation is…" When I was forty-three years old, we gave up a very successful business in California to follow the Lord. We live in South Carolina with our two teenage children. We have experienced two parent deaths, betrayal, back stabbing, being written off as a lost cause, had very little communication with family, and our friends are few. We came home to four empty rentals, our finances almost depleted, no jobs, no direction, most people we knew having moved away, culture shock, boxes to unpack and so much more.

We have had to create a new life. We have gone through trial after trial. I am doing taxes, selling houses, renting properties, taking care of my family, managing the finances and starting up a business. I understand what hard means. It is not easy, but I believe with all that is within me what I have learned and what I am learning, is what Paul is writing about. Ponder his words today in Philippians 4. Start today living each moment for Him, and focus only on today; it helps with the overwhelmed feeling that the enemy throws at you if you stick your neck out.

CONTENDING FOR TESTIMONY

As I look out the windows in our home here in South Carolina, I cannot help but be captivated by the beauty of the spring. I am in awe of how quickly everything around me is changing colors. Trees that have looked so barren since we arrived back home in December are now filling with green. Flowers are everywhere, and I am finding hope in watching them bloom. My hope is that I, too, will change seasons and bloom.

I love to learn from nature about the ways of the Lord. I firmly believe that everything around us is placed here to teach us. And so, as this season declares the glory of the Lord, I look for a message for me. I am finding one.

No secret, it has been a long winter season of the soul for me, just as the trees look so barren. But I do know that trees lose their leaves to endure the winter storms and their roots grow deeper. I, too, am finding that my roots have grown deeper in the Lord. My husband and I have felt led to start a business upon returning home to America. The business is harvesting rain water. The Lord gave us the name, "Living Water Rain Harvesting." While we were in Australia, we saw this being done, as they were in a drought for over five years. Upon returning, we found ourselves in a drought, and this is what gave birth to the business. We are so excited, and have spent the last six weeks studying and setting everything up to begin.

I received words from the Lord showing the act of faith that was being proclaimed with each tank that would be installed on the homes. With no rain in sight, we put out the tanks to prepare for the rain (harvest) that is coming, proclaiming to the Lord our thankfulness, and also, showing that we are now becoming better stewards of the water He has given us for years and we have thought nothing about. I was excited that I would get to help others, even non-Christians, prepare as well. Even though it was not what I ever imagined I would be teaching, I do see it as educating others. We have included our children in on the company, and we are teaching them both how to start a business and what it takes to run it. It has been an awesome experience. Also, when we had our business in California, we were general contractors, and rain damage cost us much money over the years. We are redeeming those days with now being thankful for the rain. I am excited to go into people's homes, and let Jesus enter with me, and help them. So many people have told us this business is going to take off, and that we are the perfect ones to do it. Excitement is in our home, to say the least.

So, with everything in place, we handed out flyers in our neighborhood introducing the company and asking people to call us. Out of sixty-five homes, we were sure that we would receive some calls. We waited and waited, and nothing happened. I asked the next-door neighbor and she had thrown the flyer away. We were discouraged. We started doubting the timing, whether we had heard from the Lord, and considered just quitting. We really thought it was going to be easy with all the things people had said, and knowing the Lord was behind it. So, what went wrong? What am I doing through this season? How do we get this business to lift off and fly? I am learning about contending.

I am coming to realize that I have to fight in prayer for this business. I have to keep telling the Lord that He gave us this business and He needs to do something. I am growing in trust. I am growing in faith. I am trusting by faith that He is doing something even though I cannot see it. I am strengthening myself in the Lord daily, and trying really hard not to listen to the enemy. Every time I look at the answering machine and it shows zero calls, I am thanking the Lord for the calls that are coming. I am walking the streets each day and thanking the Lord for what He is doing that I cannot see. I am contending. I am having mindsets shifted. I really thought that since the Lord gave us the idea and plan, He was going to make it easy for us. I was so wrong. I have to fight for it. I seek Him each day and ask Him what I am to do. One day I went for a walk, and on the way home, I thought I would write to a newspaper. In my driveway was a newspaper, and on the front page was an article about the drought and an e-mail address. I wrote to him, and within thirty minutes he responded and wanted to do an interview. We had an interview, and several days later an article with a picture about our company was on the front page of the business section. We had no idea what this was going to do for our business, but there was excitement stirring.

When I went to my first appointment and turned in my first bid, I felt the excitement of the Lord. He told me He was proud of me. It was a good day. I figured that I would receive a phone call about the bid, but nothing came. So, I just keep focusing on thanking Him for what He is doing. I stay focused on today and let the Lord have tomorrow. I really like what I am learning, although it is amazingly difficult. It feels very big. Oh, I forgot to mention that several weeks prior, we ordered seven 550-gallon tanks in anticipation of many calls. So we have spent the money and time, and now we wait. This contending tests your faith, that is for sure. I cannot wait to look back on these days of struggle and testify of the goodness of God through them. I mean it, just like the trees outside bursting forth with new life; I know we are soon going to be experiencing the same thing in our business.

Another thing I am learning is to appreciate the value of a drought. When there is a shortage of something, (such as water, money, friends, love, etc.) you are made aware very quickly of how much you value it. You have an opportunity to allow the Lord to refine your mindsets. Did you know that in a drought, grapes can actually produce better wine? Yes, they produce fewer grapes and they are smaller, but the sugar consistency is much more intense, and the wine can be award-winning in those seasons. We, again, can compare the natural with the spiritual in looking at the challenging seasons of our lives as actually having the potential to produce a better wine within us. That is what I am counting on. That is what I am praising the Lord for in this season of life. The enemy wants me to believe that we have failed, that God has forgotten about us, and that we have no future or hope. The enemy wants us to believe that we will never have a ministry and will amount to nothing. This drought season of my soul is showing me my selfishness and many other weaknesses that He is wanting to work on. Droughts in our lives cause us to dig into the Lord, if we see it that way. I choose to see it that way, every day trusting the Lord and not focusing on the circumstances, but on Him and His faithfulness. I am standing on His Word.

"Be ready in season and out of season" (2 Timothy 4:2).

I might be out of season, but I am feasting on His Word each day, and I am finding Him closer than I have in a very long time. *Yeah, God!* I was in a drought of His closeness and I pressed in harder and now I am just filled with His Spirit. Many of my circumstances have not changed, but my focus on them has. I am not saying that I have it all figured out and life is perfect, but I am saying that I am enjoying the Lord through them. I look forward to the testimony of this season. Yes, new wine! To be continued…

OUR CEILING IS THEIR FLOOR

Some time ago, my husband and I spent four months with our two children in New Zealand. At the time, our daughter was eighteen and our son twelve. We were in a waiting time, so I began seeking the Lord to find His best in it. I kept wondering and pondering this question: If our ceiling is to be our children's floor, then how do they maintain the floor and build up from there? It is like hearing someone's testimony and being encouraged, but when times get hard and you try to stand on the testimony, you fall. Think about it. We learn from hearing and watching the real thing, so we saw this time in New Zealand as an opportunity for them to learn.

What does that look like? I started with sharing my testimony with them and pouring out my heart's desire for both of them. Then the Lord showed me that we needed to be real about how we were feeling about the situation. The conversation went something like this: *Hey kids, today is Monday and on Friday we do not know where we are going to be staying, and I am scared. I feel like I have failed.* (Remember we moved twelve times while we were in New Zealand, and the Lord directed each move.) *We need to pray together and then you, too, will get to see what the Lord is going to do.* As a side note: We had a choice to just pretend that everything was great so they would not be afraid or worry, or to let them be a part of the unfolding testimony so they would know and learn what to do when they are grown and living a life of faith.

We prayed and felt that we were to go into town (we were on the South Island of New Zealand). As we got into town, a lady we met on the North Island was crossing the street. We parked the car very quickly and found her. We asked her why she was there. She explained that she and her husband had just gotten into town because they were having trouble with a rental property nearby. We sat down for coffee and talked. All four of us were really excited, and my son kept looking at me and smiling. She explained how they needed to fix some things and find someone to stay in it. Guess when it was going to be empty? You guessed it, Friday! They offered the place to us. We did the work they needed done and stayed in the most amazing place we have seen with a view of the lake and mountains and snow. See what happened? Our testimony and our faith that is contained in the foundation of their floor became a part of them. I know God does not always answer things that quickly, but He did for us.

I understand that this is different for everyone, but the underlying foundational point is still the same. I do not believe we are to hide the process between the prayer and the answer from our children. How are they going to learn? They have to learn how the ceiling got there in the first place so they can continue on from there.

We continued this processing with our children from then on. When we returned home from living in Australia, we did not have jobs, our finances were running low, and we had empty rental properties and lots of bills to pay. We could have kept this information between my husband and me, but instead we had a family meeting. I wrote down what all of our expenses were, and we began to pray for the Lord to start moving. We had an opportunity to teach our children how to budget, how to be careful with money, how to shop, and to explain and teach how the whole rental property business works. We are teaching them life principles through our daily living. It has been the most amazing time as we pour out what we know and how we think, and open the floor up to what they think. We are all working together. God is so good. No one taught my husband and I how to budget, how to look at spending and sales, and how to pray through and give it to the Lord.

I realize that everyone's children are at different ages, but if I would have known this earlier, I would have applied it at a different level. I hope it is clear what I am trying to say. They can learn from our struggles and will not be caught off guard when they are grown and have their own. Our ceiling is then their floor. Praise the Lord!

Guess what else you get? You get to watch your own faith grow as well. As you focus on how you can give all to your children, you have to look at yourself. Ask the Lord to show you what you can do with your children. If you do not have children, then ask Him how you can help others around you grow through what you are going through. It is wonderful to be a part of the process to the testimony, to take it on board and learn from it. Our ceiling (and everything contained within the walls holding that ceiling) can become an integral part of our children, equipping them to build their own walls.

BREAKING THOSE CONTROLS

What I am going to write about today could most likely rock the boats of some mindsets; I know that it sure would have rocked mine several months ago. I am digging through the ashes of the fire and journey that the Lord has had me on, and whether you feel this is right or wrong, I want to encourage you to find your own journey through this one. Well, with a disclaimer like that, you know you could be in for a rough ride, or possibly be offended.

Here is part of my background to give an understanding of the shaking. There are generations of alcoholism on both sides of my family. I was in a church denomination that did not allow the consumption of any alcohol; I liked that and had made an internal vow to never drink. I also had a fear that if I started drinking, or even tried one drink, I would become an alcoholic. So, I exercised self-control and hid behind the rules of the religion I was in for my entire life until the Lord started speaking to me about it.

We were going on vacation while living in Australia, and it was a long car ride to our destination. I had my iPod on my ears and was in my own space with the Lord, as best you can in a car with three other people. I was listening to Heidi Baker speak at the Bethel Church

(11/13/06 Iris Marriage podcast). She was talking about being drunk in the Lord. I have also experienced other people around me acting totally drunk in the Spirit. To tell you the truth, this really offended me, (actually the religious spirit within me). I wanted to avoid this part of the journey with the Lord, and I also did not want to in any way look like a total fool. Okay, I see it for what it really is, but my pride was there all the same. The Lord spoke to me and said, "If you do not give up the control of the drinking and trust Me with it, you will never drink deeply of My Spirit." I started crying and crying. My response was that I cannot do that. No way. I realized I was blocking the Lord out of a part of my life. I had an enormous amount of fear attached to the control, which, of course, was transferred into my relationship with the Lord as well. I have learned that anything that is happening in the physical in my life that I am controlling, or not controlling, is directly showing me what is happening with my relationship with the Lord (ponder that one line for a bit). So, I was controlling the drinking, and as a result, my choice was to leave God out of the control part. It is a very twisted mess of rules, laws, vows, fears, what other people have said and not said, and so many things were tied into my own control of drinking. The Lord exposed an area that was a giant within me.

I told my husband about it, and as we talked it through, he, too, had to face his own thoughts, fears and everything else about the subject. I really sought the Lord on the whole thing. Scripturally, I never could really reason through with my current thought processing why Jesus would turn water into wine, and why wine is talked about so much in the Bible. Even the vine and the branches can be associated with wine. I, somehow, would think that was for then and not for now, or not for my situation because of my history. So, we sat down and talked to our children about it, and it was quite a shock for them. But we all talked it through and decided that Wally and I would try wine that night at dinner. Oh, by the way, the drinking age in Australia is eighteen, and so now the equation of my control and fears were also focused on my eighteen-year-old daughter, Amber. The Lord had also told me not to buy cheap wine, but to get the best. We had never ordered wine before, and knew nothing about it except that it is made from grapes and comes in a bottle. We chose to purchase the best wine, by the glass. We also let our kids taste it as well. It was a family shaking and awakening. None of us liked the taste, but I had also remembered hearing that you learn to like it. (Okay, I can feel the enemy really not wanting me to write this, so I will press on.) During the next week, while we were on our cruise, we tried different types of wines.

So, through this journey of trying wine, I have really come to enjoy it. We even went wine tasting at a vineyard in Australia and learned all about vines, grapes and how wine is made. It was very interesting and brought greater clarity to other elements of the parables. Then there came the journey of letting friends who were back in the States know about it. You see, it is easy when no one around knows you. I do need to bring clarity on one other element: the pastors and leadership of the church we were going to in Australia also drank and seemed to be very free about it. At first, this really challenged me, but the shaking that resulted from them being so free about it actually moved the debris that I had in front of my closed doors of control. I did get one e-mail from a friend who explained to me that the leadership of the churches they associate with do not allow their leadership to drink. My friend also made the statement that you need to search out the reason for the drinking and make sure it is not to escape from pain.

I understood these things all too well. I would have written them myself. I am not going to deny that drinking wine casually helped to soften the pain we were going through and make it more bearable. But we never got drunk. The wine was with dinner, and we enjoyed it with our friends in Australia who had no issue with it. (I might be trying to justify my decision, which shows that the fears still need to be worked on. *Help me, Lord.*) Our son actually was excited that we were drinking, as then we fit in better. I still had a struggle with it and so was sitting with the Lord being totally honest with Him. I said, "Lord, tell me about this drinking. I am enjoying how I feel and it is easing the pain of the fire. Is it wrong?" This was His response:

"My Child, do you or others need coffee in the morning to wake you up? Is not that a dependence on a foreign substance? Is there really a difference between needing coffee and needing a glass of wine?" I could not say that there was a difference. The difference is that wine is not a foreign substance. Wine is in the Bible. Red wine is actually good for your health. That settled it for me.

I am not encouraging people to go out and get drunk with wine or anything else. However, if you are offended by other Christians drinking, be very careful not to judge them, not to put yourself better than them, and just get your eyes focused on the Lord. We are all on a different path with the Lord. He alone knows our heart, our hurts, fears, controls, and everything else. He is the Author of the timing of working on things within each of us. This is a very sensitive subject, I understand, but there is really something to what I have learned that others, too, can get free of. I do not know about you, but I want to drink deeply of His Spirit, and I want to walk in all the freedom He wants to give me. Whether you agree or not, seek the Lord and ask Him to reveal your heart in this area. Blessings to you on your journey! The ashes have been removed on this one, that is for sure. *Go, God!*

UNDO ME, LORD

One Sunday morning, I woke up with a deep longing for more of Jesus. Within everything I did that morning while getting ready to go to church, I could hear my spirit crying out to just go and worship. When I got to church, I sat down and closed my eyes, and spent some time with Jesus. When the worship started, I entered in, and at one point I was totally alone with Jesus, even though there were people all around me.

I felt my spirit asking the Lord to undo me. I just kept asking and asking the Lord to undo me. Then I saw this big tangled knot of string and I asked the Lord to undo the knots of my life. Undo the messes, the decisions, the choices, the words, the thoughts, the things I have looked at and done that have caused my life to look like that. Then, I thought about untying something that is in a knot in the physical. I seem to be the one in the home who will sit and untangle the biggest mess of a knot. It takes a long time. You have to follow one piece all the way through and loosen, pull, and untwist until what was knotted is eventually undone and usable again. I started thinking about all of my life: my past, present and future in all areas. Then something shifted within me as I pictured the Lord sitting there patiently untangling everything about me and my husband, my marriage and my children with all of our past, present and future, both together and apart. I realized that He has it all under control. He sees all of our lives from the beginning to the end. He knows more about us than we do and ever will. He is stronger, wiser, richer and more powerful, patient, faithful, kind and loving than we will ever be.

My faith shifted that morning. I stood in worship, alone with the Lord, and let go of anything I was carrying. I wanted to cry. I wanted to just worship before the Lord God my Maker, and thanksgiving came out of my mouth.

I need to remember this when the phone is not ringing for sales, when the mail only seems to bring bills, when the checking account is going down, when my children are not doing what I think they should be doing, when my marriage is not perfect and we disagree, when I am tired, hurting, sad, and just plain wondering about the future and hope that maybe God has one for me. I need to remember that God has me in His hands, and on those days when I am not feeling ever so close to the Lord, He is untangling something of my past to make way for my future. When I feel He is far away, that happens to be the day He is threading me through to the other side of my circumstances. When I feel sad or hurt, He is touching that very place in my knot to bring healing and release. Could it be that everything about me might be a knot, and the Master is working patiently each day untying all the knots I have created, or that I allowed people to create in me? Could it be He uses the circumstances of my life to position me to be undone? Oh, I could preach this one. I can feel the witness in my spirit about this.

I have noticed, lately, that my internal striving is slowing down. By internal striving, I mean the constant yearning for more of Jesus, and yet, never feeling like I am satisfied, and so I find myself in a circle of frustration. That is not of God. He wants us to enjoy every single moment that we have, good and bad. So, when I have noticed that my internal striving is slowing down, I am able to wait upon the Lord to direct my path and trust and believe what I do each day is what

He wants and needs for me to walk through for my own progress toward Him. Oh, I am not settling, but my trust in His strength when I am weak is growing. My trust in His goodness for me is growing. My trust that He knows what He is doing for my good is growing. He has me in His hand, and He loves me and has good plans for me. Is my life perfect? Absolutely not, but He is perfecting Himself in me every day.

Can you see it? We never arrive at a certain place with the Lord; we are always growing into Him. My striving was to arrive somewhere, or to look or feel a certain way. A daily walk with Jesus is day in and day out, every moment of learning, loving, trusting, seeing and believing in His love and goodness in your life. It is not about the end but about the journey to the end of this earthly life. I have always been a goal setter, organized and a planner. What do we plan for? An end, date, a what? Then you get there and you start over again. I am not saying that it is bad, as I still do plan to a certain extent, but I do not strive to complete it, and especially in my walk with the Lord, I am holding on to His hand and letting Him lead me through every day, and what that looks like for me. I trust that what happens in my day, good or bad, is for my good because He is in control of it. Remember the knot? I am finding freedom, and I can see where this path of trust is leading, straight to heaven thinking.

Help us, Lord Jesus, to be undone by You and find You as our constant source of all. May You be first in our thoughts and first in our lives. May You walk with us and talk with us through all. Show us how to walk in deeper places with You and in deeper levels of trust in You each day. May everything about us reflect You! Oh, how I love You more today than I did yesterday, and may that continue to be true of me all the days of my life. I say yes and amen to Your plans and purposes for my life. Bless You, Lord! Bless You! Open doors and close doors on my path today, and undo the knot that is in my life so that I am positioned exactly where You desire me to be each moment of each day. I love You ever so much! More, Lord Jesus, MORE!

EVERYTHING FROM GOD

I was reading in *100 days in the Secret Place* by Gene Edwards, a passage by Jeanne Guyon. Jeanne states *"You must utterly believe that the circumstances of your life, that is, every minute of your life, as well as the whole course of your life—anything, yes, everything that happens— have all come to you by His will and by His permission. You must utterly believe that everything that has happened to you is from God and is exactly what you need. Such an outlook towards your circumstances and such a look of faith towards your Lord will make you content with everything. Once you believe this, you will then begin to take everything that comes into your life as being from the hand of God, not from the hand of man"* (see reference). I have been pondering this over and over to see if I believe this or if it is really even possible.

I have observed and believe that we can get to this place, but I am far from it. I have found that when I look back after a hard situation, then I can see the Lord's hand in it, but to journey through everything each moment of my life, trusting and believing everything is from Him is not as easy for me. Why?

For one thing, when I encounter a challenging situation, I find myself blaming, discouraged, frustrated and many other things (actually similar to offense; maybe that is what is happening). I am realizing that I am first seeing the difficulties as coming from the hand of man and fighting back with everything that is within me. Not necessarily with words at a person, but internally.

For example, when we got back into the US, we needed to purchase cars. One of the cars we purchased seemed to be a problem child for the dealership. The problem was not with the actual function of the car, but with the paperwork involved. It took almost two months to get the license plates. People were getting fired and hired and messing up. They promised for weeks that it was being overnighted and I would have my plates within a day. It was a silly frustration, but time-consuming and a hassle. So, applying what Jeanne Guyon wrote above, I would ask the Lord what He was trying to teach me. It was definitely a sore spot, to say the least.

I learned that I have an internal anger within me. Why do I think that? I get frustrated. Frustration and anger come from unrealistic expectations. The Lord was working on this. I came to realize that I had many unrealistic expectations of myself and others. I had been taught this from early childhood. I thought that was what made you and others better and try harder. So, I had this battle within to let go of expectations.

Back to the question, can we look at everything in our daily lives as from the Lord? Oh, I want to, I desire to, I hope to, but can I? It must be possible, as that sure would line up with what the Lord would want. How do I do that? While pondering this, I encountered three situations in one day that rattled me. In one of them I even found myself thinking, *Lord, can You give us a break? Can someone do something for us once in a while?* This was a warning sign that I had been offended. I set it aside and said to the Lord, *I was offended. I am sorry. Please take that.*

We were trying to sell a house that we felt the Lord wanted us to sell. The people kept trying to get the price lower and lower. When we bought all of our houses, the Lord had us pay full price to bless the people, but we did not seem to be finding people extending the same blessing to us. I am sorry, but that frustrates me. My pride was wounded as well. So, the Lord was working on yet another area.

Every single day, we each walk through situations good and bad, hard and easy, and we have a choice of how we look at them. I confess, I complain sometimes to the Lord with asking for it to be easier. So much of the time it all just seems so exhausting. I believe it is exhausting because my flesh tries to survive and fights.

I want to live a life of being content with everything. Life would be so much easier internally, if not externally. I believe it is possible with God, because His Word says it is. All things impossible with man are possible with God. I say, *Yes, Lord.* If you have this all worked out already, could you be in prayer for me, please? Maybe this writing has opened your eyes to things in your own heart and mind. I pray that the Lord will hold on to you ever so tightly and help you every step of the way.

I believe Paul and others walked there. How else could they rejoice and praise the Lord in prison, while being stoned, whipped, beaten, and everything else? When I think of it that way, the silly little things that annoy me are pretty small. Paul said in Philippians that he had learned to be content, so we learn it. James says to count it all joy, so we count it joy that we are learning to be content through the process of the trials. Each trial would then be taking us a step closer to the Lord and to freedom. In Romans 5, Paul writes about developing proven character through trials. Peter writes that we add to our faith many things through our circumstances. David learned it in the caves while he was running from Saul. Joseph learned it in all the situations that he encountered. Can you see it? Many of the things they learned were from being betrayed; they had to step over offenses, walk past misunderstandings, and find the Lord in everything. The pages of the Bible are filled with the trials and tribulations and victories and defeats of God's people. Why? To help us and to show us that it is possible, giving us hope in the dark hours of the night, showing us that there is a great cloud of witnesses cheering us on to victory.

Thank You, Lord, for Your Word of truth, and thank You so much for showing and recording the bad and the good, the mess-ups and the wrong choices. We hope in You and trust that You alone know what is best for us. Bless You, Lord Jesus!

Reference: Gene Edwards, 100 Days in the Secret Place (Shippensburg, PA: Destiny Image, 2001), 152.

FACING MY FEARS

I have been noticing a change within my thinking through this time of contending for our business and this journey of my life, and I want to write about it to help others, as I firmly believe in the power of the testimony.

Where do I even begin? I have found myself continually telling others as an encouragement to step out and try, you have nothing to lose. For example, in working on getting the word out for our new business, I am writing emails, making phone calls and handing out flyers. My thoughts are that I have nothing to lose and everything to gain. I sent an e-mail the other day to a local radio station, from a lead from our local councilman, and asked if they would be interested in opening their Straight Talk program to a discussion on rain water harvesting. I briefly explained about it and just asked. If I get a response, it is fabulous; if I do not, I am no worse off, but I tried. Yesterday, I got a phone call from the station informing me that they are working on scheduling the interview. I am actually going to get to talk on the radio for nearly thirty minutes about rain water harvesting. I am excited and scared at the same time. The Lord obviously opened the door and He will help me, but I have to face my fears about the whole thing. I am in awe of Him.

Here is what my days look like: I am up early in the morning spending time with the Lord, praying over my day, my family and other requests, and then I spend time in His Word and write in my journal. After taking my son to school and returning home, I go for a walk and talk with the Lord or listen to a message on my iPod. The Lord normally uses this time to start planting ideas and thoughts in my mind about what I am to do during the day. I feel or see His direction and I move on it. He shows me whom to write to, and whom to call, and gives me the motivation for doing things. If I feel no direction from Him, I literally stop what I am doing and lay on the floor and ask Him to show me what to do.

When He does, I get back up and go at it again. He is really rocking things within me as He continually positions me to face my fears. I find myself sometimes wishing that someone else would do all this work for me and that I could just ride the wave of success, but it is me and the Lord. My husband is working for someone else while we wait for the breakthrough in the business. I know it is coming, and so I just keep seeking Him day in and day out. My faith is growing and my fears are being conquered. A new boldness is growing in me. I am facing my fears each day with the Lord. He always shows up, but I really wait for His direction and then I move according to what He spoke.

Here is another big thing the Lord has asked me to do. He has placed within my heart, and actually given me a strong vision, and spoken clearly to me to write a letter to the pastors of the churches in the area near my home and ask them to meet with me and hear my testimony. I am even to ask to speak in their churches. He showed me putting a prayer team together and showed me the paper I was to get the names from and send them out. For me, this is a really big deal and I am facing many fears, but the point is, I am facing them and not letting them stop me. Yes, I face the fear that I am a woman and no one is going to want to have me speak. Yes, I face the fear that I am a total stranger contacting them and they will not allow that. Yes, I face the fear of rejection, persecution, doubt and everything else. Maybe they will not call, but maybe they will. I know the Lord has placed a very strong desire and heart within me for the churches and people in the area, I am obeying, whatever the cost. If I write the letters and no one responds, am I really any worse off than I am now. No. But what if stepping out in faith opens a door to something that I am really supposed to be doing, and that is giving the hope and love of Jesus to others and crossing over denominational lines, and just seeing the people as Jesus sees them. That picture is what is moving me to try. I do not think about the outcome very much, other than allowing His heart for them to excite me. I feel so alive when I am teaching and writing. So, I am going to try, and if one of the pastors reading this is reading this because of the letter, then praise the Lord!

There are so many examples in the Word of this walk with the Lord. Look at the four lepers in 2 Kings 7:3-8. They had a choice to just sit there and die or possibly die trying. They tried, ate, and received riches. Really, what have we got to lose by trying, our pride? I want to lose my pride. I could even lose my fears; that would be even better. It is scary for me to approach something new, but I do know from experience that the Lord shows up when I do. How about when God told Abraham in Genesis 12:1: "Get out of your country, from your family and from your father's house, to a land that I will show you." He did not show him first. He said that He would show him, but he first had to move in the direction the Lord was telling him. The Lord does not give us the whole picture because then we might stop at the vastness of it, or take a shortcut to the end, or who knows what else we might try to do. I also believe He really likes it when we depend on Him for our every step. I am learning that.

I have also noticed recently that I have a deep hope about things. I do not remember ever having this hope before. In the past, trouble would arise and I would fight discouragement, fears and doubts, but recently something has shifted within me. Though the physical circumstances concerning finances and the business and relationships have not changed, how I view them has. I do not even recall doing anything to receive this, but I have a deep, solid hope in Jesus that is hard to explain. But, since I do have it, I also want to give it to others in their tests and trials of this life. During the last two years of my life, through the hardest and darkest times, I would, through tears say, *Lord, this hurts but I trust You. I trust that You have a good plan for my life. I trust that You are good and always are. I trust that You are faithful even when I am not. I trust You through this season of my life.* I believed with what I had and He increased it. I do not know how it works, I just know it does. When someone is upset, I have hope. When someone is hurting, I have hope. I have hope in the goodness and faithfulness of Jesus.

I want to encourage you to step out of your comfort zone and try. The desires of your heart are placed there from the Lord, so step out and try. So what if it fails or does not work out the way you thought? God will honor your trying. Think of a little child learning to walk and you, as a parent, standing in front of them encouraging them to try. You have your arms out and smile and encourage them with all that is within you, "Come on, you can do it." They take a step and fall. As the parent you do not get upset with them. No way! You are so excited and hug them and love them and tell them how proud you are of them. You encourage them to do it over and over again. Why? Because you, as the parent, know that each time they try they will be better at it, and eventually they will be walking all the time. As a parent, you know that trying is the path they have to take, and the process is one step at a time. God sees our steps of faith the same way. He gives us a vision or a desire and encourages us to step into it, and when we do, even though we are afraid, we face it and try. He loves that, and He knows that, as we try, and we experience Him showing up to help us, our faith and trust in Him grows. I have stories upon stories of God asking me to do something and I just obey and He does something amazing. It is daily for me, and He desires for it to be daily for everyone. He loves us and wants the best for us.

I give you hope to face your fears! You have nothing to lose except what you do not need, and everything to gain. One day, the Lord asked me to show up unannounced at a business at 11:00 a.m. to talk to a builder. I was scared and facing many fears. I had called and left two messages, sent a letter and had no response, and now I was going to show up unannounced. Only God! So, I went.

When I arrived at the builder's office at 11:00 a.m., the person I had been told to talk to was not in and another gentleman was not able to meet with me, but there was one man who came out of his office and greeted me. I could feel the Lord's favor as he agreed to meet with me. Guess who he was? The president of the company! Yes, I went into the president's office and got twenty minutes of his time. I was able to explain the system and cast a future vision that he could implement, and then he offered for our company to be a part of the demo home they were getting ready to build. They would take pictures during installation and insert information into their brochure and advertisement. He also said he would talk to the other builders and set up a meeting for me to make a presentation. A divine appointment and so much favor, I am still amazed at what happened! This obedience is going to change our business. I now have a personal contact with one of the largest builders in the area. All I can say is I am so glad I obeyed. *More, Lord, more!*

LOOKING UNTO JESUS

"Looking unto Jesus, the author and finisher of our faith," (Hebrews 12:2). I have been intrigued by this portion of Scripture and really like to think of it as Jesus writing my life in a book. I am the book, and as He is writing each chapter of my life, I feel it. Let me see if I can explain in simple words the complexity of the chapter I seem to be in.

I woke up one morning feeling really overwhelmed and fighting doubt, fear, discouragement, guilt and many other feelings. I kept declaring His goodness and faithfulness over my life and future. As I was writing in my personal journal what I was facing, I recognized that I was in a suspenseful or faith-building chapter. So, I chose to declare that I trusted Him with my life. My circumstances are challenging everything within me and I am finding myself thinking, *Lord, this is too hard, I cannot do this. When is this going to stop or get easier? I want a normal life with no problems or issues. I need a break from this.* He is working on many things within me at the same time and my flesh wants to eject, but I have learned that I must endure and trust and believe, because He is working on my fears and weaknesses and things that He knows are necessary for my life. Before this passage of Scripture that I started with, it talks about being surrounded by witnesses cheering us on and running with endurance. I see this as enduring through the struggles and tests of this life. Believer or not, everyone has them. I see no word *if* in that first or second verse. Not *if* it happens, it is going to happen, but He shows us what to do. We are to set aside, endure and look to Jesus. He knows the way through. He is the way, the truth and the life. He is the same yesterday, today and forever.

I will give a condensed version of the months prior that have led to this writing. I wrote in one of my writings about the letters to the pastors, and I have done that and they are all mailed. I have received two responses to date; one was a no and the other was an interest to meet in July, but the fact that I was a female and he, the pastor, was a male required that another person meet with us, namely, my husband. The fact that I understood this and he was interested should have encouraged me, but it did not. It looked hard and I was discouraged. I know that the Lord is exposing something within my heart and I am open to it. It looked hard because Wally works full-time, so setting up a time to meet presents a challenge. I am obviously being stretched, because, even as I write this, I wonder why is that so hard after what I have walked through? I also seem to be challenged and keep reminding the Lord that I am a female, and that in itself creates a challenge. I believe this is the issue He is exposing. In my e-mail in-box this morning a friend sent me a Power Point on being a woman. It is a conversation between God and an angel as God is making a woman. This was so timely for me considering my issue. I do not think I have to expand on the challenge of being a woman in these days.

Second, the business is still in the contending stage. I am planting seeds all over the place, but the seeds still are not producing a harvest (finances). I have sold one rain barrel and am very grateful, but that does not pay the bills. I did get a call yesterday from the president of that development company asking me to put together a presentation for the builders and the technical college in a couple weeks. I was excited and scared at the same time. I am going to be talking about something that we have never even done. Yes, I have a heart for rain water harvesting. Yes, I have a basic knowledge of it and understand how it works and can talk about it. I like to have the practical experience to sell it, but I have none with underground systems. I have seen the pictures and read about them, but have not actually installed or watched the installation of the systems I am selling to them. Am I crazy or what? But this is the path the Lord has me on and I must keep believing. Also, it has not rained for a couple weeks and our tanks are running low so we need it to rain, and it is so hot and does not look like rain in the future, which is good for continuing the drought. When it does not rain, people are aware of the need for collecting rain water, but they hesitate to spend the money to collect rain that is not falling at the moment. See the situation? I am speaking to people to install a system in the hope (faith) that it will rain. I cannot tell them when that will happen, or how much they will get.

There is such a parallel to the Christian walk and witnessing to others that I am amazed. I am realizing that we tend to be a people who want immediate results and do not really plan too much for the future. This is a general statement and I know there are exceptions. Our family is an exception, but in working on selling systems, this is the barrier I face. I even face it within myself as I am speaking and asking them to spend money on it. Our finances are running low and we need systems to sell. Do you see the parallel to the rain water? If it rains, people do not see the need for the system; they just turn on the faucet in their home and get water for no additional cost. If it rains, some people are open to installing the system. Either way, it is a challenge. The biggest challenge I face is what happens if it does not rain. Is this really the right question to be asking? If it does not rain, we are all in trouble. What if the money does not come in? I am facing both.

As I look at all this, I am in a difficult chapter of life that He is writing. This is the middle of the book where you find yourself suspended with every word, wondering what is going to happen next. With a literal book you have the privilege of continuing to read until you choose to stop, but when it is your very life in the chapter of suspense, it is a totally different story. Yes, a testimony is being written and established within me. Yes, my faith is growing. I so wish that I could write that this is easy. I keep thinking it should be with all I have experienced the Lord do for me, but He is obviously working on areas that were not affected by the other testimonies, and now these are being awakened. So, I choose to believe by faith for finances, for business, for rain, and for courage to keep believing and walking in the victory that is coming at the end of this chapter. He is the author and finisher of my faith and I will follow Him and be thankful.

There are many other pieces of situations and challenges intertwined within the above stories, with a daughter turning twenty today and a son fourteen going into high school. I am so very blessed and grateful to the Lord for such an amazing life. Oh, it is hard, absolutely, but the Lord is so faithful, and I look forward to writing about the breakthrough that I know is coming. Keep reading as I will. I am choosing to endure and trust the author and finisher of my faith, Jesus!

TRAIN UP A CHILD

"Train up a child in the way he should go, and when he is old he will not depart from it" (Proverbs 22:6). You shall love the Lord your God with all your heart, with all your soul, and with all your strength. And these words which I command you today shall be in your heart. You shall teach them diligently to your children, and shall talk of them when you sit in your house, when you walk by the way, when you lie down, and when you rise up" (Deuteronomy 6:5-7).

For many years I have pondered these Scriptures and tried to figure out how in the world to train up my two children in the way they should go. I would take literally the "train up a child in the way he should go," meaning that I was to take my children to church. I was to get them involved in church activities, teach them how to sit in church, have them in Christian schools, and do everything I knew that would train them up in the way they should go. The harder I tried, the more they did not like it, and I found out they were only going to church because I was making them go. They did not like it and did not want to be there. My biggest fear as a mother was that I would fail to connect them to the Lord, and that as soon as they were out of my home, they would be out of the Lord's home as well (we are still on this journey).

While we were on the journey through New Zealand, the Lord started showing me some amazing things about my heart's desire for my children. I sought Him day after day, and I do believe that through these four months of intense trial and testing of our family, the Lord used this time. I would like to share this with other moms and dads who have the same struggles with balancing work, marriage, serving in the church, and children. Somehow, we are to be training, equipping and loving our children. Information is coming at us from every single direction with teachings, books, the Word, and our heart's prayer that the Lord hears. There will be modifications depending on the ages of the children; my children were eighteen and twelve.

The first thing the Lord showed me to do was to let them see the struggles and the journey throughout the entire time in New Zealand. I was to let them know when I was afraid, hurting, doubting, lonely, and everything else. This was about the Scripture above in Deuteronomy to teach them diligently and talk when we are sitting down, walking, lying down and rising up. This is day in and day out. In New Zealand, we faced many struggles individually and as a family. We thought we were only going to be there for four weeks and we ended up being there four months, while enduring the various emails from people wondering what in the world we were doing. We knew no one in the country of New Zealand, but we had each other. The Lord showed me that as we were honest and shared our struggles with our children, they would learn a valuable thing for when they were adults. They will not be taken by surprise when they encounter a trial. We would express our situation and pray with them, and then the Lord would answer, sometimes within hours and other times days. Their faith was building. Instead of them just hearing our testimony, they were part of it, and it was theirs as well. Interesting, our ceiling is their floor, but they have to learn how the ceiling got there or they will face the potential of falling.

Day after day, we would pour out our hearts to them. We would share our testimony with them. We gave them everything we had. They really grew in the Lord through these times. We took the time to give to our children. We prayed together, we shared together, we laughed and cried, and we saw God move on our behalf. They watched as their parents would step out in faith and experience the answers to the very prayers we prayed together. It was a special time and a true gift. We may not all be given the opportunity of not working for four months and spending every second we have with our children. The point is, day in and day out we are living our testimony with the Lord, and we can include our children in it. Think about this: when we are children and are sheltered from struggles, what happens to us when we are on our own and we start encountering struggles of our own? Our job as the parent is to thoroughly equip them for every good work. This is one way to do it.

Another thing we did with our children was play trivia games (I am in no way saying that the Bible is trivia, but we can extract details out of it) about the Bible, getting them to think about it. Imagine David facing Goliath, the suit of armor, Daniel in the lion's den, and many other things. How about how many books are there in the Bible? What is the very middle Scripture in the Bible and what does it say? (Psalm 118:8) We were teaching them to look at the Word of God differently, and we gained understanding of it as well. It is really fun. I love the Word of God, and this is what I was able to give them.

We also had a week of "Fear Factor" in New Zealand. One morning the Lord dropped this into my head and so we stepped into it. We faced our fears, one being heights. Three of our family members were not excited about this height thing, but we faced it together and encouraged each other as we paraglided off of the side of a mountain with a guide. When we all reached the bottom, everyone loved it and was so encouraged that they had faced their fear of heights. They have a victory of facing and pushing through. They have a success to hold onto when they encounter the next challenge. Wally and I also talked to them one morning about how the Lord is always showing us things, and how we need to train ourselves to pay attention to everything around us. He is always giving us what we need before we need it, but we need to see it. We then took them for a walk (still in New Zealand) and got them lost. They were not really enjoying the walk up and down the hills, and they were not getting along. We kept encouraging them to pay attention. Then, when we felt they were good and lost, we asked them to take us to an ice skating rink they had seen several days earlier. They had to work together and could not ask anyone but each other where it was. Well, Amber remembered the skating rink so Jordan had to depend on her. We were amazed when they started working together. They found it and we were so proud of them. But it did not stop here. When we arrived at the ice skating rink, we gave them clues to finding the next place and they had to solve them, and also, along the way they had to pick up ten pieces of trash. We wanted them to serve the community and to learn to pay attention to their surroundings. They both seemed to really enjoy picking up the trash along the way. What Wally and I were more interested in was to see if, after the ten pieces each had been collected, they would pick up more if they saw it. Unfortunately, they did not, but it gave us a great opportunity to talk about it over coffee at Starbucks when they got us there.

The next thing we wanted them to do was serve an establishment in some way, and they did open doors for people and look for ways to serve people. Yes, we also encouraged them to try foods that they had not tried before and not to judge them by their looks and smell. We were in a country where all the food tasted very different from what we were used to, and so the food was a challenge that we all had to press through. It really opened some amazing doors for Amber, she is really open now to new foods. Jordan also is trying new things, and he had been a challenging eater. We have been totally amazed at what this time has opened up for both of our children. Our time in New Zealand pushed all of us out of our comfort zones as we learned to talk to total strangers.

We would spend evenings or mornings talking about the Lord with our children and prophesying to each other. Our son was not always so willing to participate, but we continued to encourage, help and love him. We are still continuing to do that. I am not saying that our children just stepped right into all of this willingly as we had hoped, but the Lord gave us the ideas and then graced us with the patience to walk through it with them. It is a journey through.

We are still doing things with our children to equip them. When we returned to the States, the Lord showed me that we needed to teach our kids daily living strategies. Our daughter, Amber, learned how to plan meals, prepare the shopping list, and shop for the food. She became really responsible in this area. She was working full-time, so she opened a checking account, paid rent and all her bills. She was learning responsibility for life skills. We are allowing her to find her way through, but we are there for counsel when needed. I will tell you, this was a challenge to us as parents not to step in and fix everything, but we have had to let go. We also taught our children how to start a business; we talked about all the things associated with that and they are living it. Such a valuable lesson!

With Jordan, when he was off for the summer, the Lord showed me how to talk to him about each of us having the same amount of time in a day and having a choice of what to do with it. We can waste it away, or we can get the most out of it. We have a choice of how we go from point A to point B. If point A is the bottom of the stairs and point B is the top, we can walk up, or we can skip steps to improve our heart and strength as well. So, I encouraged him to establish his own plan for each day to strengthen himself in the following areas:

— *Physical:* Some type of physical exercise of his choice. I spoke with him about setting goals and how not to set them too high, because if you cannot accomplish them, you get discouraged and quit. Set them lower at first and you can always increase them in certain circumstances, and in that way you actually encourage yourself.

— *Mental:* Read a book of interest. He needed to read each day to improve who he was. We would go to the library and let him pick out the books.

— *Musical:* Play the drums and guitar each day.

— *Internet:* Study for a certain amount of time, the stock market, banking, loans, something in the finance area. This could be combined with a book as well.

— *Service to our family:*

> — *Cooking:* Plan, shop and cook for our family at least once a week.
>
> — *Cleaning:* Clean his part of the home each week (we all split up the cleaning).
>
> — *Laundry:* He needed to learn how to do the laundry, so once a week he was to do one load. We talked about the value of learning this for when he was on his own someday.
>
> — *Dishes:* He was to choose which night he would do the dishes after dinner each week.
>
> — *Yard work:* Mow the lawns.

— *Fun or down time.*

He stepped right into this and put it on a calendar, and I was pleased with how he progressed through it. He made the choices of what and when, and that made a big difference. Amber also was included in the conversation, but she is at a different stage of life.

While we were on vacation, we had our children plan a whole day in New York together; when we would leave, and how we would get there. They had to plan the entire day; we just went along for the ride (and to supply the money). It was interesting, as they had to learn to work together with totally different views of how to approach things. I had fun, as I got to share with each of them tips on working together. What a valuable lesson they learned. They started out each wanting their own way, and ended the day working together, with Jordan giving in to something that Amber had pushed for all day.

Being the fourteen-year-old that he was, had refused, but in the end, he softened when she finally let go and he wanted to bless her. It was a lifetime of learning for them in negotiating subways, trains, buses, boats, and people; buying and working together. I was just smiling inside as I watched them struggle and find the way. This is how the Lord teaches us, as well. We were there to help if asked, but otherwise we just waited for them to figure it out. I do not know if you have been to New York City before, but it was a great lesson. Yeah, God!

So, I am learning that my job as a parent is to equip my children in every way to be all that they can be in Christ, and to be able to live in the world successfully. I hope I have articulated the amazing things the Lord has shown me, and I hope He will show you how to apply these and more to your journey as a parent, grandparent, aunt, uncle or friend. Blessings as you grow, and remember Romans 8:28: "And we know that all things work together for good to those who love God, to those who are the called according to His purpose."

GET WISDOM

I have personally been on a journey about seeking wisdom and understanding for several years now, and just last week received a deeper revelation of James 1:5: "If any of you lacks wisdom, let him ask of God, who gives to all liberally and without reproach, and it will be given to him." In the past, I had always focused on the latter part of this Scripture, mainly on asking for wisdom and that God will give me a liberal portion. For many years I have asked for wisdom every day. I have been intrigued by the book of Proverbs where over and over it is written to seek wisdom, and get understanding. I have pondered for hours what Solomon asked for after God visited him and asked him what he wanted (1 Kings 3:9). I have always felt there was something I was not understanding, and so I have been in constant pursuit of it. I will attempt to unfold the revelation how I have grasped it so far, and I am sure that in the years to come, I will have more of it opened to me.

Just last week my husband and I encountered a revelation on our current situation with our business in regard to a question we should have asked the Lord, but did not. I do not know how we were supposed to know to ask it, but if we had, things would have been easier. We were listening to a message on our iPod as we drove on our vacation, and when we heard the words of the message, we both knew. I would encourage you to download podcasts and listen to messages from other places, as I really feel it helps me to stay well rounded in the processing and learning of God's Word. I currently listen to Joyce Meyer every day, Bethel Podcasts, and T.D. Jakes, along with teachings here at MorningStar from conferences and Sunday messages. I have found all of this to be very helpful in walking this path of life with the Lord. When we realized this, I went to the Lord, as I was troubled with how in the world we were to know to ask that question (I had to make sure that I did not take offense with the Lord). Basically, He listened and I whined. When I finished whining and feeling sorry for myself, I started to see a whole different aspect of this Scripture. I noticed the word lack. If any of you lacks wisdom, let him ask of God. Before writing this, James was talking about various trials and saying that we should consider them joy because the Lord is working in us. Then, we get to the If in verse five, the backup plan, or the answer for your attitude of not counting or considering it joy. So, as I looked at it in this light, I focused on the word lack. I see this word as acknowledging a need. It is a humbling word to admit to the Lord that you cannot do it on your own, that you need Him. This brought greater strength to the Scripture in James 4:10: "Humble yourselves in the sight of the Lord, and He will lift you up." Admitting our lack positions us to receive. But what are we really receiving? Do we not really need a better understanding of what wisdom is to know that we lack it? So, then I went to James 3:17: "But the wisdom that is from above (there it is) is first pure, then peaceable, gentle, willing to yield, full of mercy and good fruits, without partiality and without hypocrisy."

I then noticed the words, *first* and *then*, which, to me, means that it is a process or a journey through a series of stages along a path to the wisdom that is from above. I love it when the Lord ties His Word together as with a rope and reinforces it for us. Let's look at the list again:

— *First pure.* It is not diluted with anything other than the purity of God.

— *Then peaceable.* As you receive this pure wisdom, you receive peace from above. It is called the peace that passes all understanding, the God of peace be with you, I, Jesus, leave you peace. We get His peace in the situation. It is one of the fruits of the Holy Spirit living inside of us. Yes, that peace is what we get.

— *Next is gentle.* It comes in the still small voice, it is offered and not forced upon us, it is easy to receive.

— *Willing to yield.* This is an interesting position I think, but I do believe that at this point in the process of receiving wisdom, we become willing to yield to the Lord's leading.

— *Full of mercy and good fruits.* I believe that we receive this so that we can give it to the others involved in what we are experiencing. We get an abundance of mercy from heaven and good fruits: thoughts, words and actions toward our situation.

— *Without partiality.* At this stage we have humbled ourselves and our own mindsets and wills about the situation and we are being transformed. So, the things we were partial to that were not correct, or that were tripping us up, are shifted, because what we receive is so pure, bringing us back to the first word in the list.

— *Without hypocrisy.* Could it be that we have an opinion about the situation that needs to be adjusted? Since it comes without hypocrisy, we can receive wisdom and allow it because we have positioned ourselves to receive it by acknowledging our lack.

After this revelation, my prayer life has changed. When I ask for wisdom, I feel myself positioned in humility to receive. I feel that this revelation has changed the word *wisdom* for me. I am even able to see what stage of the journey I am on as I ask for wisdom on particular things. I can feel when I enter the place of willingness to yield. I become willing to yield my need to be right.

So, let me encourage you, and myself included, to incline your ear to, get, pay attention to, ask for, become friends with, cherish, respect, love, and seek wisdom all of your days, because Proverbs continually instructs us to do this, and because these words came from the wisest man who ever lived on earth, Solomon. Have you ever noticed that wisdom is not one of the fruits of the Spirit in Galatians 5:22-23, but many of the aspects of it are?

Oh God, give us the wisdom from above. We want it to work in us and mold us into Your image each day! Yes and Amen!

ACCESS BANK
OF HEAVEN

With the continuing contention for our finances, business, and future, I have been learning so much, and want to try to write a part of it in hopes that it will release others as well. The testimony has much power and strength, so I encourage you to press in to this revelation for your own breakthrough and victory.

We have been contending now for several months for our business to break through, and in the process we are seeking the Lord for what to do and how to do it. When we were driving home from our vacation several weeks ago, the Lord asked me if I was ready to start fasting for Him again. I felt the anointing to say *yes* and did. This actually took me by surprise, as I had been struggling in this area for a couple years after Wally and I went on a three-day fast for a breakthrough for our visas and it took much longer to get them than we thought it would, and the fast was incredibly hard. So, when the Lord asked me, I felt ready.

He instructed me to fast every Wednesday until 5:00 p.m. taking nothing but water. I agreed and then asked the Lord what I was fasting for. He asked me what I wanted it to be for, and so I asked for a couple things. Then, He asked me if that was all, and I responded,

"You mean I can ask for more?" The Lord replied, "I did not put a limit on it." So, I asked for many more things that I have been praying for quite some time now. I could sense the Lord just smiling, as I knew that my list was increasing the length of time I would be fasting. I was excited inside, as I knew that I was finally ready, and it was going to be great.

The Lord asked me to fast on a Saturday, then on Sunday morning in church Rick Joyner gets up and starts speaking on fasting (I am not kidding) and calls the church to a forty-day fast until 8/8/08. He explains that it does not necessarily need to be from food, but rather, something that you want to get control over. As I thought about it, I wanted to stop speaking about lack. I had noticed lately that I would say many things about lack of finances, lack of friends, lack of breakthroughs, and so forth. I wanted control over that, so I decided to fast from speaking or thinking of lack. Interesting that this agreement with the Lord came the day before my husband quit his job, as we both felt that is what the Lord was asking. So, at a time when neither one of us was working, I was fasting from speaking words of lack. I felt as though the Lord put me in a situation that would challenge my fast, yet I was excited at the same time.

I started the forty-day fast on June 29 and on the morning of June 30 I started pressing in to the Scriptures that counter the lies the enemy has been speaking to me about our finances. We then got an e-mail from a friend of ours in Australia requesting support for his new ministry, and one of the items on his list was a new keyboard, and he typed the name of it. Well, we happened to have left a keyboard in Australia when we thought our daughter was returning there. We were trying to sell it. The Lord asked us to give it to him. I knew by my response that we needed to give it. I have to be honest; I did not want to give it. I thought, *Lord, we need the money. Why can't someone give us something? We are always the ones giving things away.* This convinced me even more that we needed to give it. Wally was in agreement too, so we sent an e-mail to tell our friend to go and pick it up. He was greatly blessed. After we did this, I got an enormous revelation as I sought the Lord about my heart and why He had us do this. For over thirty years we have given into the kingdom of heaven. We have heard many messages about people giving and the Lord giving back. We know the Scriptures, we have the T-shirt on giving (not bragging, just making a point). I have not been able to understand why it has not come back to us until now. The Lord showed me our investments here on earth that we have for retirement, and He showed me that they were nothing compared to our account in heaven. I started seeing the exponential growth of giving to ministries over the years, how it continues to grow, and how it can never be stolen from us or future generations. I was excited. Then, He showed me how giving this keyboard gave me a full-value return with interest as our friend's ministry for the Lord grows. If we had sold the keyboard in Australia, we would not have gotten full value, then we would have had to get it converted into US dollars and pay the fees, then we would have paid bills here on earth in the physical with the money, and all of it would have been gone. I was excited.

Then, He showed me something amazing. The fast that MorningStar is doing is for the Joseph Company anointing that is coming. Joseph was used greatly to save God's people from famine because he was in a position to collect the food (wealth) that was given to survive the famine. God was bringing an anointing to His people on 8/8/08 for what is coming in the days ahead. So, the Lord showed me that when we were in Australia and I needed money transferred into our account, I sent an e-mail to our financial planner in the US, whose name was Joseph. I would write to Joseph stating that I needed money transferred into our account by a certain date, and I also told him the amount. I used to joke with him that I was asking my dad for money. This is a true story, only God! The Lord showed me that I needed to make a request for funds from our bank account in heaven to be transferred into our account here on earth. I had not learned how to do that. I had never seen this before, so I did it and asked for money to be transferred into our account. I have no idea how, but I am asking and believing. I am excited at this and really am developing a whole new trust and perspective. We are rejoicing over any money that is coming in.

The day after Wally quitting his job and getting the revelation above, we sold our first job. *Yeah, God!* I am not going to say this fasting of not speaking of lack is easy. I have found that when I fast, all my weaknesses and wrong mindsets start coming to the surface. So, I am finding many of mine. I fight fear as I fight not to look at the physical. I fight the teachings and ways of the world that have affected my mind about being responsible and getting a job. I fight thoughts of *what does this look like to others, and is this really going to work? How in the world are we going to make it?* We have only sold the one job so far; we are trying to trust God on a level that we have not known. I have also noticed that it is much easier to give when you have money coming in, when you have a surplus. The real sacrifice of giving comes when you do not know when you are going to have more money coming in. I can really feel what the Lord is working on, and my spirit knows it, but my mind and flesh still need to die to what they believe and think. I have found myself thinking about the days when we made so much money and could buy just about anything that we wanted. I think about what it was like to have money coming in and getting a paycheck. I have actually been surprised at what is inside of me, as we let go of our business over three years ago and have not really worked until Wally started in February, but has now quit. I absolutely believe that it is what the Lord wanted, but man, the flesh is really squirming. It must die!

I have come to realize that the Lord is working in us an accountability of finances. We are being prepared for something. I can feel it. As I look at how the world looks so closely at how people in high places spend their money, I realize that the ministry Wally and I are being prepared for could go through this, too. We have to be proven in this time to be trusted and walk in integrity in the future. This stirs new strength and hope within me as I press in to what He is doing in me.

I had a dream that has encouraged me. My kids and I walk out of this building with our dog Blessing. In front of us is an eight-lane road of fast-moving traffic going in both directions. We do not have Blessing on a leash, and he runs right into the traffic. We are yelling at him to come back, but he continues dodging cars and eventually he makes it to the other side. We can hardly look as he faces so much danger, and we are sure we are going to see him get run over by a car, but we are relieved when he gets safely to the other side and sits there waiting for us. The light turns and we cross over to the other side. This was my interpretation. We knew that we were to name our dog Blessing because every time we called him we were calling in our blessings. So, when I focused on this, I was also reminded of Daniel 10:12-13: "Then he said to me, 'Do not fear, Daniel, for from the first day that you set your heart to understand, and to humble yourself before your God, your words were heard; and I have come because of your words. But the prince of the kingdom of Persia withstood me twenty-one days; and behold, Michael, one of the chief princes, came to help me, for I had been left alone there with the kings of Persia.' "

This really spoke to me of our blessings and the traffic from the enemy that they have to fight through to get to us. They make it safely through and then we cross over to get them. I have set my heart to understand accessing the bank of heaven. It has definitely been a humbling time, as we are not working, and everything I wrote about that is being exposed within me. But the Lord has heard my words, and I really feel this dream was confirmation that our blessings are coming. It has changed the way I am praying too.

I am writing this on July 17, 2008. Lately, the Lord has been giving me Scriptures for a certain date, and I still write the date as they do in Australia which is 17/7/08. Jeremiah 17:7, "Blessed is the man who trusts in the Lord and whose hope is the Lord." My hope has to be the Lord, not in the Lord, but be the Lord, and my trust is in the Lord. I am learning this as our blessings fight their way through and it is twelve more days to the date of my deposit. I do not have all of this figured out, but my spirit is at peace with it, so I am staying in step with the Spirit (Galatians 5:25).

So, I have named the bank of heaven HRIG in Christ Jesus. Philippians 4:19: "And my God shall supply all your need according to His riches in glory by Christ Jesus." I love His Word of truth and treasure greatly how He unfolds it and uses it to teach me and encourage me daily. God, You are amazing! So, my prayer and hope for all who read this is that the God of hope will do "exceedingly and abundantly above all that you can ask or think" (Ephesians 3:20). Amen!

MORE ON GET WISDOM

When I read the book of Proverbs, I have an opportunity to see how much King David valued wisdom and understanding by the words his son, Solomon, wrote. I then think of what I value in raising my children, and I know, that what we value most is what we continually feed into them. King David valued and understood the need for the wisdom and understanding that came from God. From a young age Solomon was instructed to get wisdom and understanding. He is one of the authors of Proverbs and he comes at it from every angle.

I think of my own upbringing and how, at a very young age, it was told to me that after high school was college. So, when graduation came from high school, I naturally focused on college; it was not even a choice. I went to college and graduated.

So, this journey of thought processing brought me to 1 Kings 3, where the Lord comes to Solomon, after he is king, in a dream. He does not come to him in person, as He did to Moses or Abraham. I wondered why a dream? To understand, I looked at the question the Lord asked him: "Ask! What shall I give you?" That is a pretty amazing question. The King of kings, the Lord of lords, the Creator of everything, the author and finisher of our faith asked King Solomon that question. I believe the Lord asked him that question in a dream because our true heart is exposed and able to come out in dreams. I believe that our subconscious mind is engaged in dreams. I believe that who we really are all the way through is found when we are asleep and at rest. For me, I know this is true. My flesh is not in control, and who I am to the core can be addressed. So, we know the question; now let us look at his answer. Let us start in verse 7: "Now, O Lord my God, You have made Your servant king instead of my father David, but I am a little child; I do not know how to go out or come in (acknowledging lack of wisdom, as in James 1). And Your servant is in the midst of Your people whom You have chosen, a great people, too numerous to be numbered or counted. Therefore give to Your servant an understanding heart to judge Your people, that I may discern between good and evil. For who is able to judge this great people of Yours?" He asked the Lord for what Solomon was remembered for, getting wisdom. David had prepared his son to get wisdom above everything else. So, even in the depths of who King Solomon was, remained the desire of his heart to get wisdom.

I, then, would have to wonder, if this was part of who he was, then why would he need to be asked in a dream? Would his flesh have asked for something different? Would ours? Would his flesh have tried to reason and think it through to get the most of the question? Most of us have encountered the story of the genie who gives you three wishes. I know for myself, when I was younger I thought about what I would ask for, and then my last choice would be to ask for more wishes. So, our flesh can have a tendency to be selfish. I think you understand the point I am making. How does this apply to us?

This has caused me to consider what I have been putting into my children. What do I feed into them? What should I not be feeding into them? It is an interesting journey to walk through. If the Lord came to them in a dream and asked them this very question, what would they ask for? For that matter, what would the Lord find within my heart? I know the Lord works on my heart in my dreams. I have many dreams that reveal what is within me. He uses dreams to bring to the conscious mind what we have pushed away and forgotten. I wake up many mornings thinking I did not realize I was still bothered by those things. I repent and ask the Lord to bring healing. While the Lord is working on my past and what is deep within me, I have to pay attention to what I am putting back inside of me. What am I reading or not reading? What am I studying, listening to or watching? If He is working on getting the dross out, I need to work on the part that I am responsible for now: my mind, my heart, my spirit, and my emotions.

It is a journey through to the deeper things and freedoms in God, and I am pursuing them with all that is within me. This is my prayer: *Oh God, I personally lack wisdom and need Your wisdom in everything. Lord, may my heart of hearts seek You in all. May You fully and completely abide in, dwell in and inhabit all of me. May nothing be untouched by You. How I love You and trust You through all. Thank You for revelation and for Your love for me. Bless You, Lord! Amen.*

THE MIRROR OF THE PAST

"Therefore lay aside all filthiness and overflow of wickedness, and receive with meekness the implanted word, which is able to save your souls. But be doers of the word, and not hearers only, deceiving yourselves. For if anyone is a hearer of the word and not a doer, he is like a man observing his natural face in a mirror; for he observes himself, goes away, and immediately forgets what kind of man he was. But he who looks into the perfect law of liberty and continues in it, and is not a forgetful hearer but a doer of the work, this one will be blessed in what he does" (James 1:21-25).

I have read this passage of Scripture many, many times, and have always heard it to say that I needed to do what the Word of God said to do. I thought I had been doing this for nearly thirty years. I really thought I understood what this Scripture was trying to communicate until one day the Lord gave me a very clear picture of verses 23 and 24, which are underlined above.

I was in the process of converting all the videos of my children growing up to DVDs so they would be preserved. It is a very big project, and I have wanted to do this for at least five years now, but just had not known how to do it. I had actually carried much guilt about it, as I had heard that the tapes break down and you eventually will lose them. These tapes are from the very beginning of my children's lives until now. The Lord showed me how to do it and I am in the process. Watching these videos has been very eye-opening to me about myself. I am actually observing my past, or a part of it. I have observed how controlling and protective I was. I can see my selfishness, as I only wanted the videos to be about Amber or Jordan. I am only up to Amber being five and Jordan just being born, and I do not like what I am seeing. It is not fun to expose my faults, but I want to be free.

First, I noticed that by desiring to focus attention only on Amber or Jordan, I missed an opportunity to capture other family members interacting with my children. Some of those family member have died and it is no longer possible. It has opened my eyes to the relationships that I no longer have with family. I have found myself, over the last few years, wondering what I have done, and blaming them for all of the distance. Through my own hurts and misunderstandings I seem to have done exactly as the Scripture above has stated, "observing his natural face in a mirror; for he observes himself, goes away, and immediately forgets what kind of man he was." I forgot what kind of person I was. Since the Lord graced me with the opportunity to view my recorded past, what am I going to do with it? Do we really forget so quickly what we do each day? Does offense really get us to focus only on the other person and totally forget or discount or rationalize or justify our own reactions, words, and behaviors in each situation? From my experience, it does. As I listened to people close to me interact with me and my children, the very things I did not like, I heard myself doing and saying. I think you get the picture. I sure did!

What am I doing about it? I am choosing not to stop at verse 24 where the sentence ends with *was*, I am continuing to *but*, which is in the next verse. Usually when we hear that word, it is used in an "excuse" sentence. But I am choosing to look into the perfect law of liberty and continue in it, and I am choosing not to be a forgetful hearer but a doer of the word, because this one will be blessed in what he does. I am writing to each person the Lord shows me and apologizing for my actions and lack of actions, and focusing on reconciliation with family and friends. It is a slow journey through, and I have to be patient and really submit to the Lord, as my flesh wants to rise up. For my part, I am focusing on the fact that, most likely, I have forgotten what I have done or said, and have hurt them as well. I am trusting the Lord one day at a time through all of this. He is working a good testimony within me, but it is a test, that is for sure. I am not responsible for their response back, just for my part in all of this. Part of me is excited at what the Lord is showing me. This is the truth that sets us free.

This has also brought me to Hebrews 12:12-15: "Therefore strengthen the hands which hang down, and the feeble knees, and make straight paths for your feet, so that what is lame may not be dislocated, but rather be healed. Pursue peace with all people, and holiness, without which no one will see the Lord: looking carefully lest anyone fall short of the grace of God; lest any root of bitterness springing up cause trouble, and by this many become defiled." That one is a fun one! So, I am on a journey of pursuing peace with the people in the past, and along with that, pursuing peace with people in the present. I want the video of my future to look totally different from the one from my past that I am now observing.

I do want to insert a caution statement here. The Lord has prepared me for this. I had listened to messages about this and thought no way, until I heard a message from Kris Vallotton, of Bethel Church, talking about the Lord confronting him on reconciling with his sister after all these years. My thought at first was, *No way Lord,* and then I said, *Okay, Lord, but You will have to change my heart to do that.* I submitted to His hand to prepare my heart. This is the only way I can write that I am sorry, and that my heart really is clean and not filled with hidden agendas. It also positions my spirit to be humble and accept whatever the response or reaction is. My trust is completely in the Lord. He set it up. But with this caution comes an opportunity for the reader to ask yourself what you would observe if you watched a video of your life. If you think too quickly that there is nothing there, you might want to watch some videos of the past to make sure. This revelation has really changed me. I had no idea how my life affected other people. God is so very good and kind to allow me to pursue peace with people. I am getting free as I pursue and look into the perfect law of liberty and let His Word abide in, dwell in, and inhabit all of me.

HE PRUNES OUR BRANCHES

"Every branch in Me that does not bear fruit He takes away; and every branch that bears fruit He prunes, that it may bear more fruit" (John 15:2). I have heard this Scripture for many years about Jesus being the vine and us being the branches. Teachers and pastors have come at it from every angle there is, and I thought I understood the spiritual and natural implications of the passage completely. I love to prune trees and bushes and I find that the Lord really speaks to me when I am pruning things in my yard. I understand the physical need and value for pruning.

Let me see if I can clearly explain this revelation that has deeply affected me. As we abide, remain, continue, and stay in the Vine (Jesus), our real self comes out. Through the trials and tests of our lives, the good and the bad are revealed. We understand the bad to be the dross that must be removed so that the pure silver or gold within us can be brought to the surface. This dross could also be associated with the branches within us that are not producing fruit. As we look at a grapevine, we see that there is one main vine with many branches coming off of it. I always thought that each branch was a person. But if you look at it as each branch being a part of you, then you see this passage of Scripture in a whole new light.

A vine dresser removes the parts that are dead and not producing fruit. This is done in the natural, because these parts that are unnecessary draw strength or nutrients from the rest of the plant. So, you remove the dead wood and non-producing parts to create a stronger, healthier main plant. Relating this to our spiritual walk in abiding with Jesus, He, too, needs to remove the parts within us that are not producing fruit, or even the ones not producing the fruit we were created to produce.

Then, when we come to the next part, we see that He also prunes parts of the branches that are producing fruit. Why? So the branches can produce more fruit. This is what encouraged me. The Vine dresser, our Father, also has to prune the gifts and talents that He has given us. When we find ourselves in a place like the one I am in right now; where we feel that all of our talents are not being maximized, is when we see the pruning He is talking about. Our gifts and talents need a pruning from season to season so that they will produce more fruit. I saw this as a time when our gifts and talents become submitted to Him. We find out within ourselves if we have them in the wrong place, or are relying on them in the wrong way. When our branches that produced fruit in the past are pruned, we can feel worthless, not useful, washed up, too old, and all the other lies the enemy tells us during this season to get us disconnected from the Vine. The enemy wants us to feel like it is all over. But what is happening is that we are being given an opportunity to get closer to the Father in the process. It is a gift from the Vine dresser to humble us. I have found this to be true in my own life as I wait, believe and hope for a future.

I have been encouraged to know that what was producing fruit in one season will produce even more fruit in the next. We need to go through seasons of pruning. Can we really learn to embrace these seasons? Can we really "count it all joy" (James 1:2)? I believe that all things are possible with God, and so the answer is yes.

In a short study of grapevines and pruning instructions, I also read that for the first year you are not to prune a vine, but to allow it to grow wildly. Then, the next year you determine where the strengths are and begin pruning for an ultimate picture of a vine, one cut at a time. Part of the pruning is also training it to grow as you tie it up to a wire. I know in my own life when I encountered the filling of the Holy Spirit over six years ago, the first year was amazing. Then the pruning began, and it has been a journey ever since. For three of the years, I had some pretty bad days, and could not even get out of bed at times. But, I have become stronger in the Lord through it. As the bad branches within me are removed, I am finding such a deepening of my faith, a new confidence in who I am in Christ and who He is in me (abiding). I am welcoming, most of the time, His trials and tests that I find myself in, and am finding the fight not quite as hard as it used to be. Praise God!

As we press in to the abiding presence of Jesus each day, we will encounter the work of the Vine dresser upon our branches within. Embrace His touch with open arms, because He really knows what is best for us, and He sees the whole picture of our lives. He knows our path and the plans He has for us. He knows what we need and what we do not need. *Oh, Lord, we say "yes" to Your pruning of our branches, and we thank You for Your wisdom and skill in doing it. Bless You, Lord. We love You!*

BLESSING IN OUR HOME

It has been no secret in our home that for many years I have neither liked dogs nor wanted a dog in our home. When Jordan was little, we did get a dog, but it came with lots of conditions, and it also came totally trained, and was past the puppy stage. My family had to take care of him and he was their dog. He was a big dog and I tolerated him. He passed away before we moved to South Carolina, and since then I have not wanted another dog in our home. Honestly, I did not like the way they smelled, licked, and shed, the mess they left in the yard, and the responsibility they bring, not to mention the expense. I think you get the picture; I did not want a dog.

During our last few weeks in Australia, I woke up one morning feeling that I wanted a small dog. I was shocked. Only the Lord could have changed my heart and mind. I kept thinking within myself, *Why do I want a dog?* When I announced to my family that I felt we were going to get a dog when we got back home, they were all shocked. I had an excitement within me that I did not understand.

When we returned home a week before Christmas, I really felt that we were to get a dog, a puppy even. I knew what kind I wanted, so, on Christmas Eve we went looking. The Lord had also given Jordan a dream that showed him what the dog looked like, so we went on our treasure hunt to find the dog. I knew his name would be Blessing. The Lord told me that every time we would call his name, we would be prophetically calling in our blessings. At the first pet shop, I looked at all the dogs, and knew it was the wrong place, so we went to another. At the next one, I was using my discernment to determine the temperament of the dogs. I saw the puppy that was to be ours, and I just stood there. Then Jordan proclaims that it is the dog in his dream. When they told me the price I started to cry. I felt silly for crying over a puppy, but I could not hold back the tears as I looked at him. I did not want to spend that much for a dog, but something inside of me knew that this was the dog the Lord had planned for us. He brought immediate joy to all of us. He has such unconditional love for each of us that it is amazing.

So, why in the world am I writing about a dog? Well, I have learned many lessons about the Lord from him. The first thing I have been abundantly aware of every day is how excited he is to see us. Jordan said it best when he said "every day is like Christmas to Blessing." He greets us like we had been gone for years, even if it was minutes. Is this not how we are to love the Lord? I have challenged myself to have this type of excitement and love for the Lord every moment. I also see that this is how the Lord feels about us. Just look at the Bible, it is full of parables and illustrations of this.

He also loves everyone, whether they want anything to do with him or not. He really loves people and is not shy about it. Is this not how we are to be in the world around us? What if everyone loved each other the way Blessing loves people? He gets all excited and just wants them to love him; and he loves them back. He captures everyone's heart, whether they like dogs or not. Do we love others that way?

He loves to hang out with me. He follows me from room to room. At times he even sleeps on my desk while I am working. If I move to another part of the room, he moves there too. He loves me whether I say anything to him or not. He just wants to be with me. It has been a healing to me to be loved and accepted at this level. If any of us are having a bad day, he just loves us and gives us that look that tells us everything is going to be okay. Is this not what our relationship with the Lord is to be? I do believe this is how the Lord loves us; I just want to love Him back the same way.

When he was little, I would take him for walks with me. He would not leave my side at the beginning, so a leash was not necessary. But as he has grown and his curiosity has grown with him, a leash became a needed piece of equipment to keep him safe. The first time I put the leash on him, he fought it with everything within him. He twisted and turned and pulled and resisted. I just kept walking with him on the leash and telling him that it was for his protection. Eventually, he stopped resisting and we went for our walk, and it was great. I realized that this is what our walk with the Lord is like. He knows what is best for us, but we resist at times because we do not understand. I knew that when Blessing accepted the leash, he would get to go on a walk with me every day and he loved that. What do we miss by resisting the protection or correction of the Lord? This has taught me to trust the Lord even when I do not understand what in the world is going on.

He is gentle and loving all the time. When I am going to take him in the car, he is always willing to go and does not ask where we are going or how long we will be gone. He just wants to go. I want my relationship with the Lord to be like this. I do not want to question everything, and evaluate and reason each thing. I just want to go when He says He is going. Is this not what Jesus modeled for us when He was here on the earth?

The other morning, as I was pondering all that I have been learning and receiving from Blessing, I wrote this to the Lord:

— I needed a companion on my walks to encourage me to do it every day, and You gave me Blessing.

— I needed a compassionate heart, and You gave me Blessing.

— I needed to smile and laugh more, and You gave me Blessing.

— I needed to learn and see unconditional love, and You gave me Blessing.

— I needed to learn about Your wisdom and understanding, and You gave me Blessing.

— I needed someone to just be with me and be quiet, and You gave me Blessing.

— My family and I needed healing, and You gave us Blessing.

— His name is an accurate prophetic word for what he truly is to our family, a blessing.

So, the Lord uses whatever He wants to teach us, model for us, and help us understand who He is. We have the choice to see it and grow into it. He is always teaching and speaking, and I am enjoying and loving the ways He chooses to show me. He is an awesome God and I love Him so very much. We have Blessing in our home! *Amen!*

GIVE ME, LORD

The other day I found myself praying in this way: *Lord, help me not to be excessive in anything either way, in what I do, how I see, and how I think. Give me an understanding heart.* When I said the words, *Give me an understanding heart,* they really dropped into my spirit. I pondered that and kept saying it over and over. So, I want to write about my revelation of what an understanding heart is.

I went back to what it was that King Solomon asked for. He asked for an understanding heart, not for wisdom. Again, in Proverbs, wisdom and understanding are always linked together. In Proverbs 4:4, King David instructs his son Solomon, "Let your heart retain my words." He did not say mind; he said heart. Then, when the Lord came to Solomon in the dream, what was in his heart was to get understanding and wisdom. We are instructed in Mark 12:30: "And you shall love the Lord your God with all your heart, with all your soul, with all your mind, and with all your strength." Heart is first in the list. In the physical, our heart is what keeps us alive; if our heart stops, so do we.

As I pondered what an understanding heart would be like, I thought it would be a heart that has compassion and grace for others. It is not judging or critical. It is patient, wise and gentle. To me, an understanding heart is what the Bible is continually communicating to us over and over in so many different ways. Jesus had such an understanding heart, and He was our example (1 Peter 2:21-25). The Word continually talks about forgiving, not judging, not being critical, being patient, wise, gentle, and about the fruit of the Spirit (Galatians 5:22-23). Can an understanding heart really bring us to a place where we can actually walk in the ways of the Word? Could it be that an understanding heart brings us to a place of wisdom because we know when to speak and when to listen (James 1:19). We know that we are not always right, and therefore, we are not so quick to judge others (James 4:12, Matthew 7:1), and extend grace (Ephesians 2:8)? Can an understanding heart actually give us the capacity to pray for our enemies (Matthew 5:44) and pursue peace with people (Hebrews 12:14)? Could it be that an understanding heart keeps us from being critical of others and from gossiping about others (1 Timothy 5:13)? Can an understanding heart open up the Word of God, and give us ears to hear and eyes to see? Could it be that an understanding heart gives us a greater capacity to love and give grace? Could it be that an understanding heart gives us understanding of humility, and truly give us the character of Jesus? The likeness of Jesus toward others? Is this why God was so very pleased with what King Solomon asked for when He came to him in that dream in 1 Kings 3? Does this explain why, when Scripture unfolds, it strengthens and encourages us with an understanding heart? I do believe that the answer to all the above questions is YES!

Look at Proverbs 3:5-6: "Trust in the Lord with all your heart, and lean not on your own understanding; in all your ways acknowledge Him, and He shall direct your paths." Proverbs 2:2: "So that you incline your ear to wisdom, and apply your heart to understanding." Proverbs 7:4: "Say to wisdom, 'You are my sister,' and call understanding your nearest kin," You keep family in your heart and you love them. Just as our heart keeps us alive in the physical, an understanding heart keeps us alive in the spiritual and keeps us connected to Jesus.

What would this do to your witness in the grocery store when the line is long and you are in a hurry, and the person checking the groceries is in no hurry at all? What would this do to the person who betrayed you, stole from you, lied to you, or hurt you? Would an understanding heart change our view of the world around us, and also, the view of the world about us and our Jesus? I do not know about you, but I am heeding the words of King David to his son to get wisdom and to get understanding. I am going to keep asking the Lord for an understanding heart. I am going to keep studying and listening to His Word so that it becomes who I am. Years ago, I told the Lord that someday I want to only speak Scripture to people when talking to them. I have come to realize that this is a very big thing to ask, but yet, I do believe that it is possible. I desire for His Word to dwell in (Colossians 3:16), inhabit, and abide in me (John 15:1-10), becoming the very essence of who I am (Hebrews 4:12), one day at a time.

The other day a friend sent me a book for my birthday; it was titled *Qualities of a Spiritual Warrior* by Graham Cooke. On the back cover were these words, *"Warriors do not react to their circumstances, they respond to God. They see everything as an opportunity to learn, grow, advance and increase faith. They have taken their own internal territory. They do not avoid tough situations; they are not looking for rescue. They are developing a revelation of God, so profound; it governs every facet of their lives. Warriors know that Jesus reigns and everything leads to majesty. That means that every situation is not theirs to win; but theirs to lose. In this book, Graham Cooke examines the qualities of people who fight from victory not towards it. He explores the attributes required for involvement with God at a high level of warfare. Warriors cannot be intimidated by the enemy, because they are too busy being fascinated by Jesus"* (see reference).

I want this to be who I am. Oh Lord Jesus, may this be who we all become. Give us an understanding heart so that the things of this world, and the lies and schemes of the enemy, have no effect in our walk. May this be who we are day in and day out, just focused on You! Open our hearts to a deeper revelation of an understanding heart and Your love today. We love You more and more and thank You for the greatest time on earth to be alive and living for You! Yes and Amen! I just love the relevance of His Word.

Reference: Graham Cooke, *Qualities of a Spiritual Warrior* (Vacaville, CA: Brilliant Book House, 2008)

AMAZING GRACE

Not long ago I was up in Maryland speaking from my heart to a group of people. I was sharing from the journey I have been walking with the Lord. I got to one area of our finances, and I realized I had hit a wall in my faith. I want to write about my journey through that wall and know that there is grace in my testimony for others to walk through their own situations.

A while back, I wrote about the bank of heaven, contending for our business, and my forty-day fast. On my journey through our finances, I had come to a place where I was paying our Visa bill with our equity line to buy time for our business to start up. As I sought the Lord about this, He showed me that I was still doing this in my own strength. This actually scared me as I thought of the earthly consequences of paying the Visa bill with our available cash. We pay everything on Visa to get mileage, so it is a large bill each month that we pay off. I realized I could learn this with being obedient and not using the equity line, or I could continue to use the equity line to pay the Visa bill and max it out and still be in the same situation, and have no money and a large debt. Now for those of you wondering why in the world I am using my equity line to pay my Visa bill, it is less interest and a tax write-off at the end of the year. It was my own way of treading water. As I was sharing this, I thought, *I do not think that I can have the faith for this. I do not think I can run completely out of money and have enough depth within me to trust that God will provide.* As I spoke to those people, I felt that I had failed or was going to fail. I thought, *You have asked too much of me, Lord. This is my breaking point. Oh no!*

When I finished speaking, I sat down and found a speck of faith within me to say to the Lord, *I know that I have hit a wall in my faith, but whatever faith I do have, I give it to You. I have no idea how to walk through this, but I am choosing to trust You to help me and show me the way through.* It took me several days of repeating this over and over.

Also, in the journey of the Lord exposing whatever He wanted to during this season of stretching my faith in finances, He showed me that I was not paying the tithe on our rental property monies. I was seeking the Lord in this area of our rentals, because with every one of our rental properties there has been a continuing struggle with rent payments. Even this very month, each tenant was not able to pay their rent on time (while I was fasting from speaking of lack, I might add). This is a fun one to write about, but here goes transparency. I had reasoned in my head that we did not owe any tithe since the properties were not producing a positive return each month, and also, we had many months of no rent, additional costs, and many other issues. I do not believe I had ever given it a thought as to whether I should or should not pay the tithe over many years. So, when the Lord started opening up this area, I had a struggle within. To me it was looking like I was back to paying on the net or gross of a paycheck. The fact that I even had to think about it, or struggle with it, pointed me in the direction that I needed to do it. So, I was faced with paying the tithe on rental properties that were not covering the costs. Again, I gave this to the Lord for His help and grace to do what I felt He was asking me to do.

Here is the testimony part: After returning home from Maryland, I did not feel the burden of the finances anymore. I submitted to paying the tithe on the rental properties, and within two days of returning home, we signed a large project, and also, sold two rain barrels. This brought in a large portion of the money to pay our Visa bill for the month of August. The bill will be paid, and we did not go further into debt. God did it.

He had also told me on August 10th that in ten days from now a door will open. It will seem like a small door, but go through. Yesterday, I woke up in anticipation of this open door, as it had been ten days. Out of the blue, a one-sentence e-mail from a builder I had not heard from in nearly two months, appeared. He asked if I could meet with him the next day. I saw that open door and I stepped through it. I was really excited, as I had tried and tried with him and I could not get anywhere with him. All this time later, he emails me. Only God!

Late in the afternoon yesterday, he emails me again and wants me to have all sorts of information that I did not have prepared. I just gave it to the Lord. I knew that He set it up and so He had to do it. One of the main things that he requested was a marketing plan. I got up early this morning and asked the Lord for the marketing plan and He gave it. I was so excited. I knew that I had the anointing to go into that meeting. When I was sitting in the waiting room, the Lord said to me, *Last time you knocked on the door uninvited, but this time you have been invited in and they want to hear what you have to say.* I could hardly wait for the meeting. They started the meeting telling me I had thirty minutes, but after the meeting started and the Lord was giving me prophetic words to speak over their futures, I stood over an hour later and they were very open to working with our company. The meeting was not about them using our company; it was about the future of water and what their part was in it. I did not say that the Lord showed me this or that. I just spoke into their situations using words that only could have come from the throne of grace and were applicable to their current situations.

I have learned that I just have to open myself to the Lord on a situation where I internally hit a wall and He does the rest. I do not know how it works, but I do not have to. I give Him what I have and submit to Him working it all out without my help. He changed my heart, my fears, my concerns and my circumstances. I sent out an e-mail this morning to some friends and I want to include a portion of it here, as it will bring freedom.

I want to share a revelation, because I believe there is grace for everyone who reads this to receive breakthrough in what they have been trying to get free of for some time. I believe the grace from the Lord is this: Whatever it is that you have been crying out to the Lord for to change within you, submit it one more time to Him and it will open up a trickle of water from heaven to bring the river and flood to release it from your mindsets and life. This has happened to me. Just believe by faith what I am writing; breakthrough is attached to these words. It is not by accident that we harvest rain water. Water is vital for life. It moves things easily, makes things weightless, brings cleansing, loosens hard things (for instance: something is stuck to a pan and you soak it in water). Water also brings refreshment. The grace is for the mustard seed faith to believe one more time for thought processes to be moved and shifted with the living water of heaven dripping and flowing over them. (The name of our business is Living Water Rain Harvesting. Whoa!) May the Holy Spirit bring the understanding and release to each of you in the name of Jesus. May finances and ministries be released in the name of Jesus. Lord let dreams, hopes, struggles, fears, mindsets, behaviors, worries and concerns be released in the name of Jesus!

I have learned that He does not want us to struggle, fight, and have to figure everything out. In Isaiah 55:8 we read, "For My thoughts are not your thoughts, nor are your ways My ways, says the Lord." If His thoughts are not our thoughts, why do I spend so much time trying to figure things out? I really believe that we just have to submit what we have to the Lord, and resist the devil and he will flee. It might not happen or change overnight, but I can testify that change within me continues to happen, and I have no idea how. Only God! Grab this for you. *Yes and Amen!*

FAITH WALKING

For the last several weeks, there have been two words continually running through my spirit: faith walking. Not a faith walk, but faith walking, which would imply to me a constant forward motion that continues with each step. To explain further, I will walk through the last six weeks.

It started with a journey across the United States to take my daughter Amber to ministry school in Redding, California, at Bethel School of the Supernatural Ministry. It was a wonderful time with her and we talked through challenging situations. I almost felt like this was the last days that I, as a mom, really could give her the last pieces of my ceiling to support her floor. I will cherish the time we had. I miss her, but the Lord has graced me so strongly that I just stay focused on the fact that it is exactly where the Lord wants her to be, and so I stay with His plan for her life. So, through the phone calls of struggles and homesickness, I encourage her that she is going to make it, that I love her, and that God has a good plan for her. I am simplifying the conversation, but He has really graced me with a supportive role and I am not sad. Oh, yes, I want to fix the roommate struggles and the hurts and the pain that is coming from the work the Lord is doing, but I pray and receive peace from the Lord and keep going. I am so grateful. She is in an amazing place and has the opportunity of a lifetime before her, and so I am excited for her. Yeah, God!

Besides the main focus of the trip, the Lord had other encounters for me to press through with Him. On the driving part of the trip, I would receive phone calls, and one in particular from a friend who was really struggling. I continued to encourage her in the Lord and tell her that He has a good plan, and I would pray. The friend had to move out of where she was living and needed a place to live. The Lord had very clearly told me no before she asked me. In fact, He told me the same thing at least four or five times. My flesh felt sorry for her, and I would have asked her to live with us if I had not heard the Lord's response. But something inside of me believed that He had a perfect place for her to live and I needed to stay out of the way. Well, the day came that she asked, and I had to explain to her that the Lord told me she could not stay with us. I did not totally understand at the time why He was saying that, but I knew I needed to obey no matter what she thought of me. I also knew that if I had not obeyed, neither of us would have His grace upon our lives to make it through any situation. She was most likely offended, as it would have seemed very logical for her to stay with us, as we have a separate guest house and need our home cleaned, and someone to cook would be fabulous, especially since that is what Amber did for our family. But I still had to obey the Lord. I really had to fight through guilt day after day. She has not called me since, but I have heard that she is living with a family and it is working out very well for both sides, and that blesses my heart for all of them. It was interesting to press through the flesh within me and just listen to His Spirit guiding my steps and words.

The next challenge was meeting up with my husband's family, with whom the Lord had me on a journey of reconciliation for several months prior. I was excited and nervous at the same time. I purposed in my heart to really hear them, listen to them, and ask them questions whether they asked me anything about me or not. I really sought the Lord, and again, He graced me with an amazing time with his family that I could never imagined could have happen. Let me tell you, this has been an extreme struggle for our entire marriage of twenty-six years, and with this one meeting, my heart has completely changed. I have enormous love and compassion for them that I never thought possible. The struggle I had with them for all these years was gone as we cried together and shared and apologized to one another. It was the most amazing God-filled day of reconciliation that I had ever experienced. I walked into the situation holding on to my Daddy's hand and He showed up. It was wonderful for my daughter, too. Such a breakthrough! It started several months ago when the Lord had me write letters to them, and the meeting was just so good. I cannot even express it in words. I love them and care deeply for them as never before. Yeah, God!

Another extremely challenging situation presented itself with a person with whom we were staying. My husband was telling me we had to get out. But something inside of me felt that we needed to stay and press through. I prayed and sought the Lord each day as I encountered a person who was quite angry with me. I just kept seeking the Lord and trusting Him. On the final day, I asked the Lord to please make a way for four areas to be discussed. We were in the last two hours of our time in the home, and the Lord showed me how. I started with apologizing, with humility, and the doors opened for every area to be discussed. When it was over, I was so amazed at what the Lord had just done. As much as I did not want to face the situation, the Lord graced me with courage and strength. He did not do it for me, but He sure helped me through the situation. Again, I am amazed.

When we arrived in Redding, it was challenge after challenge with Amber's living situation and the terms and conditions involved. I sought the Lord over and over again for His plan through this. I was only going to be there for a week to get her settled. Finally, some extreme circumstances arose, and I felt very strongly that I needed to find her another place to live. Every door opened in one day for her to have a new place to stay and share with two roommates. The hardest part was letting the other landlord know of our decision. I really had no idea how hard it was going to be, but again, I held on to the Lord's hand and He walked me through it. I encountered a very strong spirit of control while talking to her, and the Lord showed me how to avoid every snare I encountered. I never challenged her, I never complained about her, and I was not interested in her opinion of my decision. Basically, the decision was made. I am really simplifying the situation. I was amazed at the work the Lord has done within my heart over the last three years as I heard her say not very nice things about me and my daughter. They did not seem to faze me, and the Lord helped me press through. This was really, really, really big for me.

Amber was settled and by Saturday I was on a plane heading home. I was just in awe of what the Lord had walked me through. But it was not over yet. I got to the airport in Chicago at 9:00 p.m. and missed my plane because we did not leave San Francisco on time. There were no more flights out of Chicago to Charlotte that evening, so I walked the journey through the airport to the customer service counter with all the other people. There were weather delays and the line was very long. Everyone was saying they would not give a hotel room because of weather delays. The longer we waited, the angrier and more frustrated the people got. I was in line for at least one and a half hours. I purposed in my heart to trust the Lord. I just kept rejoicing over what He had already brought me through. I was not going to agree with anger, or fear, or discouragement. I asked the Lord to please get me a hotel, as I did not want to spend the night in the airport. I was tired, and it had been an enormously long three weeks of pressing through and picking up victory after victory. So, when it was my time to talk to someone, I very nicely stood there and explained why I missed my flight. He told me some things and there was an exchange of kind words back and forth, and then there was a pause and I waited. Then he said, "If you do not tell anyone, I will give you a hotel voucher." I agreed with his terms, and again, I was ever so grateful for what the Lord had just done. I did not have to argue, push, and yell or anything. My Daddy took care of me again.

I am coming to realize that each day of my life is a day of faith walking. I sit here today with our finances still challenged and our business not totally supporting us. Just this week, after paying our tithe on Sunday for all of our rental properties and other miscellaneous income, my computer stopped working. I really had to fight not to question the Lord and not to be offended again, with Him. I chose to trust Him through it. My computer has my whole life on it. I have a backup, but it would take many hours to put everything back together, along with the e-mail addresses, and many other things that would be lost. I think you understand; it was big to me. Again a struggle with my flesh, but I chose to trust and believe Him. I got my computer back on Wednesday and it is working fine. It had eight viruses and they were all fixed. Praise God! The Lord had told me He had it taken care of, but something within me was not sure exactly what He was meaning by those words, but I trusted Him with any result. I am seeking the Lord to find out if there are viruses within me that are affecting my spiritual walk and that will cause me to shut down someday. I see this as little things that happen or that I choose to do that let the enemy in, and they work as viruses against my faith. He has actually shown me a couple of them, and I am trusting Him to fix them.

So, I find within my spirit the hope of breakthrough for our current situation. I wrote in my journal: *I am feeling like something is going to break open soon. That will be so good. Thank You, Lord, for the breakthrough. Lord, in the physical I keep thinking we should be running out of money and yet we are not. My flesh keeps thinking it has to run out, and yet, my spirit feels You are taking care of us. I do not understand how it is working, but we are in the tenth month and again our Visa bill is paid. There is no dramatic testimony of a check in the mail, or of money appearing miraculously in our account, or of a bill mysteriously paid off; but the money does not seem to be running out. Christmas is coming and I feel in my spirit that we are to have a normal Christmas. It is really a struggle between my flesh and spirit on this. My flesh wants to figure it out, and my spirit is trusting; it is a day-to-day trusting faith walk. I do not know how it is working other than that I arise and seek You, and choose to trust that You have each day. I trust that*

You are in control of every moment of my day, both good and bad. I know You have a way through the struggles, hurts, and everything else. At times, I frustrate people around me, with waiting on You, and yes, I have to fight through the possibility of looking stupid, but I am willing to fight through the frustration of others to hear from You in some way. Somehow, I know You will show me.

Could each of us be like the blind man in Mark 8:22-26 who told Jesus he saw men like trees walking? Do we see things in ways that they are not? Trees don't walk! Yet, he believed, and Jesus put His hands on him again and he was healed. Is faith walking a moment-by-moment trusting that God is good and is in control no matter what it looks like? I think so. I know so. No matter what the circumstances look like, I have come to learn to trust Him. It is a choice to trust Him even when you cannot see to the end of the situation, even when everything in the situation hurts and you desire so desperately to escape the pain. I am still learning that choosing to believe and trust in Him is the way through. I have been and still am learning to be led by Him in any way He wants to lead me: by words, by His Word, by a feeling in my spirit, by a vision, by a dream, or by knowing. I just want His plans and purposes in everything. I look for Him in everything. I expect to see Him in everything, and I do, though not always right away. Faith walking is a constant walking in a forward direction even when the trees appear to be like men walking.

ENTER WITH THANKSGIVING

"Enter into His gates with thanksgiving, and into His courts with praise. Be thankful to Him, and bless His name" (Psalm 100:4). This morning, I cannot seem to stop meditating about being thankful. It is pulsing through my veins, heart and mind. Several months ago, early in the morning the Lord woke me up and said, *My child, you have become thankful.* I was really pleased and thanked Him. Over two years ago, I purposed in my heart to be thankful about everything. When things around me were not going as I would like them to go, I found a way to be thankful for the things that were. Sometimes I really had to search and make myself focus on even the smallest thing to be thankful for.

Having a thankful heart and mind brings freedom, as you can enter into His gates. What will you find beyond His gates? We will find peace that passes understanding, wisdom, fullness of joy, hope, direction, understanding, purpose, love, and Him. Our Creator, Who knows everything about us, and Who knows the perfect answer every single time, is there. We have the greatest Father ever, who always has a good plan and purpose for us. He has a future and a hope for us. He is our life. Could this be why life and death are in the power of the tongue? We speak thanksgiving and we enter into His gates. We speak words that are negative, critical, and judgmental and we get death. If our Lord is the way, the truth, and the life, then it seems to me, especially in these troubled times, that we need to work at being thankful. I have personally found it to be the best mentality to have.

We can be thankful while waiting in a long line when the clerk is struggling and everyone around us is frustrated. Thankful for what? I am thankful that I have the finances to buy the things I need, and that I have the freedom to purchase it. I am thankful that I am healthy and have a hope living inside of me. I can see the line as an opportunity to just be thankful. The line is a place of waiting and redirecting my focus. Sure, I have a choice to join everyone else in frustration, but where does that get me? I want to enter into His gates, and standing in a line is an opportunity to enter. You cannot really do anything about the poor clerk except pray for him and smile and be thankful. That changes the atmosphere around you.

We can be thankful for everything, even with the headlines of today's paper talking about banks in trouble around the world, presidential candidates criticizing each other, the stock market the lowest it has been in four years, unemployment up, jobs hard to find, earthquakes, deaths, explosions, messes everywhere in the world, and gas stations here in South Carolina with no gas at all. Yes, I sit here today with all of this going on around me, and our own circumstances in the physical not all that great, and yet, as I focus on being thankful, there is a hope in the darkness where I cannot see. There is a flame of His hope within me. So, I choose to be thankful for my health, for my home, that my bills are current, and that I have a bed to sleep in. I am thankful that this season will pass and a new one will come, even though I cannot see it at all. I am thankful that the Lord is doing a good work in me through the struggles of day-to-day life.

I am also thankful for the future and the hope of my children through the struggles of their daily lives that want to tear my heart apart, and yet, I stay focused on His plan and purpose for their lives no matter what it looks like right this moment. I speak life words into them when fear is surrounding them. When they see no way out of their situation, I cannot help but think that if I do this for my children, my Father in heaven does this for me. I think about how it blesses my heart when my children say "thank you," or when they are so excited and are blessed and tell me about it. I love it, and just want to rejoice with them and give them more and encourage them. If I, an earthly person, can get such pleasure from this response from my own children, what does God the Father get from my rejoicing and believing Him through all? Oh, my heart is so thankful. Being thankful is a purposed choice in every situation and every circumstance.

If I am having struggles with my husband, my children, or another person, I purpose to focus on things to be thankful for. I have to really work at this one sometimes, but when I really focus on my husband's faithfulness to our marriage and taking care of our family, or the positive things in another person's life, then the bad and irritating things become less troublesome. Could it be that I am again entering His gates? I continually look for opportunities to speak to the Lord.

One morning, I was driving in the car and just thanking the Lord for the ability to teach. I have a hope within me, deposited by Him, to teach someday, so I thanked Him for it. I love to write and hoped someday to be writing books. I thanked Him for that desire, as I know that He gave it to me. I was wanting to thank my Daddy for how He made me, and what He is doing in me, and express my love to Him. My flesh wants to struggle with this and say that I am not living in the real world. The flesh tries to say "your business is not producing income to pay your bills and your savings is going to run out, there are no jobs and you will be out of money soon and then what, the stocks are falling, the economy is crashing all around the world, there is trouble all around you."

In spite of all the bad the flesh tries to throw at me, my spirit rises up and says, "Don't fear, God is with you." I choose to focus on being thankful for what I do have and for what is good. I have my health and there are people in this world struggling to stay alive. I have a home and there are people in this world living in cardboard boxes. I have food to eat tonight while others are going hungry day after day and have no hope. I have Jesus and He is enough for me, and I am thankful for Him. I am thankful for how He made me, and that He has a good plan for me.

We started a 1,000-piece puzzle the other night, and as we opened the box and dumped all the pieces on the table, it seemed impossible to put so many pieces together to create the picture on the box. But with one piece at a time, it is coming together. I cannot help but think that the Lord looks at our lives just like I am looking at the puzzle, and then He begins and continues to put together our lives to create a beautiful picture. The manufacturer of the puzzle put all the pieces in the box and gave the picture, just as the Lord created us with everything we need to get through what we are walking through today. How can we not be thankful? Oh, my heart is filled with thanksgiving, and, for me, that is the way through all of this perceived mess around me. Rejoice! The King of Glory, strong and mighty, is on your side! "Let this mind be in you which was also in Christ Jesus" (Philippians 2:5). All the fruit of the Spirit is within you; allow it to become who you are, and allow it to filter your circumstances in all. *To God be the glory! Be thankful to Him, and bless His name.*

A CHEERFUL GIVER

The other morning, I woke up fighting a bit of discouragement, and so I approached the Lord to ask Him what was going on inside of me. I have been on a journey with the Lord creating in me a clean heart (Psalm 51:10), and He has, yet again, showed me a deep level of my heart that He wants clean. It had started the day before when I was signing our tax returns to get them in the mail. I looked them over and felt a bit hopeless, but tried to push the feeling away.

As the Lord opened my heart, I saw that I was comparing our tax returns with returns of the past when we had our business. I realized that, in the past, I took a great deal of pride in looking at our returns and comparing them with the year before, and being encouraged by the increase in income. I would even go so far as to graph our income each year. I repented of the pride from the past that I saw in my heart. This time I was discouraged because for the last three years they have been going lower and lower, and this one was negative. I felt a bit like a failure, and yes, worthless in the eyes of the world. So, I gave that to the Lord.

That was not all the Lord showed me. The day before, I was listening to a message from Bill Johnson, and he was talking about how he is excited and grateful to get to pay taxes. That really stood out to me, and I knew I was anything but grateful to pay taxes. Then, of course, the next day I got my tax returns in the mail. I had been pondering Bill's comment, and as I looked, I saw that while we had our business, I looked for every way not to have to pay the taxes we had to pay. I remember many times I would be so upset when we paid our estimated taxes every month, but at the end of the year we would still have to pay a very large sum of money. I remember saying that the government did nothing to get this additional money and we worked very hard for it, and so much of it goes to them. (This is fun to write about!) The Lord reminded me of the Scripture in Matthew 22:21: "And He said to them, 'Render therefore to Caesar the things that are Caesar's, and to God the things that are God's.' " I am sure that, at the time, I had every excuse and rationalization in the book why I did not owe the government any more money. As I really looked at this with the Lord, He reminded me of 2 Corinthians 9:7: "So let each one give as he purposes in his heart, not grudgingly or of necessity; for God loves a cheerful giver." Surely He did not mean paying taxes, did He? Of course, He did not stop with that Scripture, He went on to Philippians 2:14-16: "Do all things without complaining and disputing, that you may become blameless and harmless, children of God without fault in the midst of a crooked and perverse generation, among whom you shine as lights in the world, holding fast the word of life, so that I may rejoice in the day of Christ that I have not run in vain or labored in vain." *Lord, You do mean all things. I want to become blameless and harmless in the midst of this crooked and perverse generation that takes great pride in avoiding paying taxes.* I repented before the Lord for my attitude over all those years of paying taxes with an ungrateful heart.

As I am writing this, I can see that I have not been all that grateful in paying sales, property, or any type of tax. *For that Lord, I am so sorry and admit my wrong attitude and ask for Your forgiveness. I receive Your forgiveness and ask that You help me in the future to pay with a grateful heart.*

He did not stop there. As I thought about our retirement money that is losing thousands by the day in the stock market, I saw that although it was totally legal, my motive for putting the money into retirement was to avoid paying taxes on it. I would put the maximum allowable amount away ever y year with the total motive of avoiding taxes. Yes, it is for retirement, but when retirement is twenty or thirty years away, it is not the true motive. I, again, repented for my wrong motives and heart attitude. Did we really save anything when we are now faced with withdrawing from the retirement early and paying all the penalties, and then taxes on top of that? I really repented and saw my evil ways. It was interesting that these were the ways of the world and it was totally legal, but my attitude and motives were totally wrong, and really, if I was not writing about it, no one would even know. These are some of the ugly hidden things of my heart.

I could not help but then repent for the times I had given at church not having a cheerful heart. The times I thought, *One more time they are asking for money,* and so I would give. I repented for the times I gave in the offering, knowing I was going to get a tax break because of it. *It is really ugly, I know, and I am so very sorry, Lord.*

I am amazed at how the influences of the world can twist and shift how we see things and actually condone choices that we make. I cannot help but wonder if our economy is in the condition it is because so many people have been like me and hated paying their taxes, and did not appreciate the government for what it does. Could it be that our economy is reaping what it has sown? (2 Cor. 9:6) *Oh God, I am so very sorry, and I admit to and repent for paying my taxes with a very ungrateful heart over the years. Bless our government, I pray.*

I am grateful for the deep parts of my heart being revealed, and I feel free from the choices made in the past. I will pay attention to my heart and continue to press in to Him, allowing the truth of God's Word to wash over me and set me free. He showed me my heart with a word from a message. I am so thankful for His love and timing and how He instructs us daily.

HOPE FOR
A SUDDENLY

L ately, I have found myself in a waiting room. To me a waiting room is a place in my life where I do not seem to be going anywhere and I am finding myself wondering what my purpose in life is. I look at prophetic words that have been spoken over me and our family; I have dreams and words that I, personally, have received about the future from the Lord, and yet, those words, dreams, and hopes seem to be nowhere in sight. Most days I cannot even figure out how they could ever come about, and so that is what I define as a waiting room. In a doctor's office you sit and wait for your name to be called. It is usually quiet and you are just waiting.

While in this waiting room, I thought I would write about what the Lord is showing me, and about how I am finding hope in His Word. I have determined that I am out of season at the moment, and the Word clearly states in 2 Timothy 4:2: "Be ready in season and out of season." So, I am readying myself daily by reading His Word and studying it, I am praying and spending time with the Lord, I am listening to messages and reading books and writing. I am looking into the future of my life and seeing no doors or roads to take, so I have to press in to the Lord for hope.

I have found the word *suddenly* running through my head day and night. I want to believe that everything can change suddenly. I want to believe that He has a good plan and purpose for my life. I kept hoping for a "suddenly" in my current life, but when you can see nothing there, it is a bit of a challenge. The Lord began to bring passages of Scripture to my mind, and showed me many of the "suddenlies" in His Word. They have been placed there to show me that miracles still exist, and to give me hope for my "suddenly."

He first showed me Moses, and I thought about him tending sheep in the wilderness for his father-in-law day after day for forty years, thinking that he had failed after being in the palace. Could he have even imagined what would happen next? Did he have prophetic words to look to? Did he have something burning inside of him that he wanted to do? Did he just think this was going to be his life? Then, he came across a burning bush that was not being consumed. I am sure he had seen many burning bushes in the desert, but something was different with this one. It was a 'suddenly' for Moses. His life was totally changed.

What about Saul? He was sent into the mountains to find his father's donkeys, he encountered Samuel the prophet and was anointed king. Is this what he had waited for all along? Had he had dreams and visions? He was going about his everyday life doing the best he could, unaware of the suddenly he was about to experience.

David was tending his father's sheep when he was called into the house and anointed king by Samuel. He was still a young boy. Could he have even imagined being king? Did he wonder, while tending the sheep, what he would do with his life? Did he see a future? He did know the Lord and did grow in the Lord out there in the fields. He got a "suddenly."

Solomon was raised to be king, and he goes to bed one night, has an encounter with God in a dream. The next morning he is the wisest man around. That looks like a "suddenly" to me.

Esther most likely desired to get married and have children. Could she have thought of what her "suddenly" was to be? Could she have even imagined that she would be in the king's palace and be prepared to be the queen?

Rahab the harlot desired a better life, and she had heard of God. Did she feel trapped? She would look out that window; what was she looking for? She then has a "suddenly" moment and hides the spies, and her life is forever changed.

We cannot forget Joseph. What must it have been like to have a dream and then be thrown into a pit, sold into slavery, and thrown into prison? How did he hold on to his prophetic word? In every situation he was in, he grew in favor. He walked in blessing everywhere and in every situation, and yet, he was continually wronged. Then one day, his "suddenly" came and he was ready.

As I move to the New Testament, I think of the disciples. One day, while they are doing their normal everyday task of fishing, Jesus walks up and says to follow Him and He will make them fishers of men. Is this what they thought would happen? Did they even dream of this? Yet, they had a "suddenly" moment and everything for them was changed.

Of course, we have to go into Acts 2, with those waiting in the upper room. Boy, did they get a "suddenly!" It even states the word suddenly prior to describing what happened. Every one of them was never the same again.

I also think of Mary, Jesus' mother. She sure had a "suddenly" one night. Just this young girl thinking she is going to marry this carpenter named Joseph, but then she has a visit from an angel and her life was never the same.

Then there is Paul; he sure had a "suddenly" on the road to Damascus. Once again, he was going about his life, and then, everything was suddenly different.

As I have continued to ponder this whole "suddenly" word that the Lord has given me, I cannot help but be encouraged. I can see that, while I am in the waiting room of my life, I am being prepared for my "suddenly," and also, the Lord is working on my "suddenly" at the same time. Yes, there are the arguments within my head from the enemy saying that my "suddenly" is never going to come. But, I have to believe the Lord has a plan and a purpose. I have to believe that He is preparing me for the fulfillment of my prophetic words and dreams. His Word is very clear about giving me the desires of my heart, in Psalm 37:4. Jeremiah 29:11 tells me that He has a future and a hope for me. If you are in the waiting room, you know the Scriptures that you cling to, but He has now given me a common thread laced throughout His Word from start to finish of hoping for what I cannot see. Looks like faith to me (Hebrews 11:1). He would not have so many examples in His Word, if it were not for such a time as this.

You can find hope that God is doing a work in you, no matter what situation you may find yourself in. Through the frustrations, betrayals, offenses, lies, cheating, hurts, disappointments, and everything else, you can hope in His Word in you, and hope that He has a "suddenly" down the path for you, too. How long? Only God knows. We know that He is very patient and very precise, and He will not set us up to fail. Even if you look at your life and think everything is a mess, or you have made wrong choices and feel that it is too late, let me encourage you today to let hope rise up, and believe with that last breath that He has a plan for whatever season you are in. Submit to His plan through the pain and disappointments, through the perceived successes of others ahead of you, and allow Him to complete the work He is doing in you. Press in to Him through this season, and refuse to give up on Jesus Christ, the author and finisher of your faith. Remember that Jesus Christ is the same yesterday, today and forever. He did the "suddenlies" then and He will do them forever. *Amen!*

GOODNESS
OF THE LORD

"I would have lost heart, unless I had believed that I would see the goodness of the Lord in the land of the living" (Psalm 27:13). I have been pondering this Scripture and have come to realize that this is what I do in my everyday life; I look for the goodness of the Lord in the land of the living. The "land of the living" to me is everything around me; my life, my husband's life, my children's lives, friends, family, neighbors, everything in the land that I live in.

For me, this has evolved through my journey into another Scripture passage, and that one is Romans 8:28: "And we know that all things work together for good to those who love God, to those who are the called according to His purpose." This Scripture passage starts out with *And we know*, which to me, means this is within our capacity to understand. By looking for the goodness of the Lord in every situation, we position ourselves for the possibility of finding it in the land of the living. When I personally encounter difficult situations, I try to stop my emotions, overreactions, and thoughts, and I start looking as quickly as possible for the good the Lord has in the situation. I tell myself the Lord knew this was going to happen, so there has to be something good in it. So, instead of the enemy taking me out with negative thoughts, I look for the path of good the Lord has planned for me.

I believe we have to have an expectation of the goodness of the Lord in every situation, and then He will reveal it to us. I am not meaning in any way that the circumstances change immediately, but my perspective on them shifts pretty quickly. Then I can see the Lord's solution, because "We know that all things work together for good to those who love God, to those who are the called according to His purpose." I love God, and I am His workmanship created in Christ Jesus (Ephesians 2:10). Because of this, I believe in the goodness of the Lord in every situation.

As we position our thinking to this possibility and expectation, we find hope, and are standing strong in the Lord by allowing Him to move in our circumstances. When I took my daughter back to California at the end of August, this was put to the test within my everyday life and also in my daughter's. We had many opportunities to position ourselves to look hard for the goodness of God in the circumstances, and we did over and over again. I still, daily, have this opportunity, and He does bring good into every situation of our lives. This is something I am teaching my children to look for too.

The other way this has invaded my land of the living concerns my response to things the people in my household are walking through. My daughter is also walking through challenging days learning to live so far away from home. I have found myself, many times, positioning myself to be the peace in her storms of life and looking for the good to speak to her in them. I happen to have a gift of encouragement, so the Lord uses that very much. I am not saying that I can always immediately position myself in this way, but this is the place I need to be in order not to get caught up in the storm. When my daughter is wronged and hurt, I really have to hold on to the Lord, and trust that He has a good plan through all of this, for both of us. It is getting better and happening quicker each day that I purpose to walk this way. Again, it is a choice to walk each moment with an expectation of the goodness of God in everything. If we do not, we will lose heart, as David wrote.

This has been a very valuable gift that the Lord has given me to understand and grab hold of, especially in the circumstances of the world around us. Lately, I have found myself saying something that a friend said to me in Redding, California, "When you are squeezed, you find out what kind of juice you are made of." So, I am paying attention to the juice that is coming out of me in my daily circumstances, and I want positive words. I want faith, trust and hope to pour out of me to everyone I encounter. I want to walk and breathe 1 Peter 3:15: "But sanctify the Lord God in your hearts, and always be ready to give a defense to everyone who asks you a reason for the hope that is in you, with meekness and fear." I see the circumstances of our nation right now as an enormous harvest field for us to walk in the hope and joy of the Lord, and for the lost to see it in our daily lives and inquire of the hope that is within us. While our nation is being shaken, we do not have to shake with it. We are on a firm foundation and that will not be shaken. We get to be the chosen vessels to help the people around us to see the goodness of the Lord in the land of the living.

I do believe that Psalm 27:13 is a very appropriate Scripture for the times we live in, and that is: "I would have lost heart, unless I had believed that I would see the goodness of the Lord in the land of the living." I would like to encourage you to look for and expect to see the goodness of the Lord in the land of the living around you today. No matter what it looks like, start believing this for yourself and for the people around you. It is already within you and it will make a difference. God is good all the time. May the laborers rise up for the harvest that is before them! *Yes and Amen!*

HE GAVE HIS WORD

The other morning, I awoke with a thought from the Lord that is shifting my faith and changing how I think about everything. The thought was this: *Lord, You gave Your Word.* This seems so simple, and yet, for me, it has been profound as I have thought about what that really means. In the world around us, when we really want someone to trust us or believe us, we give our word. We do everything we can to convince them to believe that we mean what we are saying. I have even heard people say that they swear on a stack of Bibles that they are telling the truth, and this is supposed to get us to believe they mean what they are saying. In movies and on TV you hear people say they give their word that they will do what they say. There is great value in that statement as long as they stick with what they have said. So, when the Lord dropped into my spirit that He gave His Word, I felt the weight of it.

Ponder that with me for a moment. He is so sure and confident and faithful in His Word that He had it written down, and His Word has endured. He gave His Word to us, knowing full well that it would be misunderstood, taken out of context, twisted and distorted, and used to hurt many people in their walk with Him because of wrong interpretations. Think about it; would you do that when you give your word? I know, for myself, that if I give my word to someone and then they misunderstand it or use it against me in some way, I am prone to defend my word, or try to bring clarification. At times, I can even find myself questioning words that I have given. What about the times when we make absolute statements to our children in the heat of the moment. I have had challenging times with my children, and I have found it a more common occurrence as they step into their teenage years and challenge what you say or have said.

The Lord does not waiver or change His Word, His Word has stood the test of time. He gave His Word that He would supply all our need according to His riches in glory by Christ Jesus (Philippians 4:19). He gave His Word that we can do all things through Christ who strengthens us (Philippians 4:13). He gave His Word that in all things we are more than conquerors through Him who loved us (Romans 8:37). He gave His Word. He gave His Word that He would never leave us nor forsake us (Hebrews 13:5). He gave His Word to us so that we can trust Him and believe Him through all. He gave His Word to me in Psalm 139, assuring me that He created me and that He is with me. The next time you open your Bible, think about His Word to you. We can trust Him. We can believe His Word. Is this what the men and women of the Bible knew? He gave His Word, He made covenants that He kept, no matter what.

I cannot help but look out the window and see the sky, sun, trees, animals, and everything within my sight, smell, hearing, and touch. It is amazing to me that He gave His Word and they were created. He spoke in the beginning and it is all still here, just as He said.

I can also see how the enemy has used the circumstances of our lives to get us to doubt and not trust this, because we, as humans, break promises or words that we speak. How many of us were raised by parents or people who broke promises? They meant them when they spoke them, but because of things happening or whatever the circumstance, they let us down. We, too, have done the same thing, or at least I have. I can see this as something the enemy has done for generations, working on each of us to break our word to others so that it hinders our trust in His Word to us. I think of when I stood at the altar across from my husband-to-be, telling him that for richer or for poorer, in sickness and in health, I will be there with him. I will remain with him until death do us part. Those vows have been tested many times, and I praise the Lord that for twenty-eight years they have stood. But in our society, these words have often been broken, and the fabric of our trust gets affected too.

When we give our word, there is weight to it; whether we want to believe it or not, it is there. How many of our words could be written down and we stand by them for thousands of years? I, personally, would think after one generation the words would be forgotten, but He gave His Word for generation after generation all through history. He gave His Word. This is changing my faith. For this time right now, the depth of His faithfulness is establishing something deep in me. My prayers are different; the way that I look at His Word is different. He gave His Word to be there for me and you. We can really rely on, stand on, believe in, and trust in His Word to us.

Maybe this is yet another reason why there are so many Scriptures about the mouth and being careful about what we say. Could it be that through the obedience on our part in these Scriptures we are spoiling the plans of the enemy to continue to chip away at the trust of His Word to us? I think it could be. Commitments we make, promises we give, doing what we say we will do are all standing on our word to whomever we have given it. When we accept to work for our employer, we are agreeing to be at work on time and give a full day's work each day. When we buy a house or a car and get a loan, we are giving and signing an agreement that we will pay it back. When we write a check, we are promising that the money is there in the bank to cover it; otherwise, the other person would insist on cash. What about our commitment to the Lord when we receive Him as our Savior and into our heart? What about when we promise someone we will do something, or be somewhere and we do not show up or do it? Does our understanding of His Word to us affect our word to others? As followers of Jesus Christ in the world around us, this should be a shining difference. As followers of Jesus

Christ, we should be always true to our word, on time, obeying the laws of the land, paying our bills, and staying married. We should be the best employees, employers, neighbors, friends, spouses, children, parents, etc. Is this possible? If we try to do it in our own strength it is impossible, but not with God's enabling; for with God all things are possible (Mark 10:27). His Word in us is worked through us. Our faith in His Word enables us to trust, love, believe, and be who He created us to be. So much seems to be falling into place, I can almost see it as Scripture after Scripture pulls together.

Is this why the disciples could be beaten and thrown into jail and still praise the Lord? Is this why we read about the men and women in Hebrews 11 and their faith walk? Is this what they knew? Did they understand the surety, strength, truth, and faithfulness of His Word to them? Absolutely!

My brothers and sisters, He gave His Word, and we can absolutely and totally trust in His Word through every second of every day. He gave His Word to us in Romans 8:28 and Romans 8:38-39. He gave His Word to us from Genesis 1:1 through to Revelation 22:21. He gave His promise, and we can believe Him. *Yes and Amen! Thank You, Lord!*

OPEN UP THE DOORS

"And now abide faith, hope, love, these three; but the greatest of these is love" (1 Corinthians 13:13). I was pondering this Scripture this morning as I was thinking of putting together a Christmas letter, since it is that time of year. I have used this Scripture before in a letter, but this time I saw it in a different light and wanted to share my journey through the three doors represented in this Scripture.

First, I saw a door of faith. We are encouraged to share our faith with others, and we all have different interpretations of what that looks like. With some it is easy to share our faith; with others it is more challenging, even when we call ourselves Christians, with others of different faith, there is yet another level of challenge.

I was holding a Bible study in my home, and one week we pondered the Scripture in Romans 12:3 that says each of us has been given a measure of faith. Every single person on this earth since the creation of time has been given a measure of faith. How big is that measure? What does a measure even look like? In my heart, I feel like that measure is what each of us needs in order to believe in God. He set it up that way for each of us to have faith in Him. (I would like to encourage you to do a search of all the Scriptures pertaining to the word, *faith*.) So, if we all have this measure of faith within us, why doesn't everyone have the same faith? Why do churches struggle to get along with each other if we all have the same faith? Or is it the same? Hebrews 11:6 tells us: "Without faith it is impossible to please Him, for he who comes to God must believe that He is, and that He is a rewarder of those who diligently seek Him." This would be a reason He gave each of us a measure of faith. But what happens to that "measure" when hard times come? Can all the troublesome situations we encounter affect that measure of faith that He has placed within us? Is it possible to increase our measure of faith? Do the cares of life cover faith or keep it hidden and not allow it to grow? Is it that mustard seed? I believe the enemy works very hard at keeping that measure of faith within each of us from growing. How does it grow? By reading the Word of God. Romans 10:17: "So then faith comes by hearing, and hearing by the Word of God." By spending time with the Lord, we get to know who He is, especially by praying, reading books, listening to messages, pursuing the Lord and getting more of Him inside us. We can allow His thoughts, His wisdom, and His abiding presence to dwell in each of us. As we do this, we receive healing from the hurts of the past, from wrong mindsets, choices, and everything else. His Word, then, starts to grow within us and become our filter. We know this, but the enemy really has covered that measure of faith with layers of stuff. The Apostles asked Jesus (Luke 17:5) to increase their faith, so we, too, can ask Jesus to increase our faith.

We open this door of faith to the people around us by being Jesus to them; looking for ways to serve, give to, help out, and love them right where they are. Could our choices actually help uncover the layers in others to allow their own measure of faith to find the daylight and grow? Absolutely!

The next door is hope. We can open doors of hope to the people around us in this season and in the seasons to come. A bad economy could be scary for many without hope. Hope looks different to each person. To Christians, hope is in Jesus. To others, hope is in a paycheck, job, bills being paid, in their healing; the list is endless. But one thing is for sure, we all need hope. Ask the Lord to show you how to give hope this season. Maybe you give hope to someone by inviting them for a cup of coffee and listening to them. Maybe you give hope by sending a check, giving a kind word, a smile, or mowing the lawn for a neighbor. Hope can take on different forms for everyone. Open doors of hope to others.

Then, there is the greatest door of all, the door of love. I have found that as I am getting older; I am gaining new understanding of this word and what it means to others around me. This year, for me, has been a year of reconciliation with family, as I have written about. But as I have also walked through the experience of a daughter going away to school and all the feelings and emotions of what that brings, I am gaining understanding of what my own parents went through. When I was in my twenties, my life was focused on me and what I was going to be and do. I really did not give much consideration to what that was like for my mom. As I find myself looking forward to the day of having grandchildren to love (which is a few years down the road), I see how much love my parents have for our children (their grandchildren). I now see how decisions I made have possibly hurt the heart they have for my children.

Our little dog also has opened a new door of love and compassion that I did not even know was possible. Such unconditional love he gives day in and day out. This door of love the Lord has been opening within my heart is expanding so that I can open it to others. Yes, the door of love will look different to each person, but I am finding that it is part of the treasure hunt of life with the Lord, discovering how to open doors with others and how to keep them open in relationships. It starts with His work on my own heart, and with me allowing His love to fill me. Relationships open up when we are more interested in the person for who they are instead of what they can do for us. Love has to be allowed its work in us first. Give what you can and be open to more each day.

As I look at all three of these doors, I see that they are all interwoven with the love of Jesus. They are three and yet one. Sound familiar? As we allow our own measure of faith to grow within, we are able to give our faith, give others hope, and give love to all. May we take the time daily to see opportunities and begin opening these doors to family, friends, and then to strangers.

May I encourage you to ask the Lord to increase your faith, and show you any possible door you have closed through the years, and then put a new doorknob on the door, and a welcome sign, and try again to give hope and love to others. Jesus stands at the door and knocks. Are we willing to answer? I close with Mark 10:27: "But Jesus looked at them and said, 'With men it is impossible, but not with God; for with God all things are possible.' " Doors of faith, doors of hope, and the greatest of these? Doors of love.

TWO BAGS
BEFORE US

Recently, Wally and I encountered a challenging situation with our finances. Wally went to work for a Christian builder and worked for two days. He was then told that he had to wait for three weeks to get paid, as that was when he, the builder, would get paid. We waited until the date that he said, but heard nothing. Finally, Wally was able to reach him on the phone, and he said that he had not gotten paid so he had no money to pay him. Through a series of phone calls and emails, nothing has come of those two days of hard work.

As I sought the Lord about the situation, to get my heart and attitude lined up with His, He gave me a vision. I saw before me two bags of seeds. One of these bags was filled with seeds of anger, revenge, bitterness, resentment, deception, and all the other things with which the enemy uses to steal, kill and destroy us. The other bag was filled with seeds that looked the same, but these were seeds of life, hope, joy, prosperity, grace, love, goodness, kindness, patience, and everything else that the Lord came to give us in abundance. John 10:10: "The thief does not come except to steal, and to kill, and to destroy. I have come that they may have life, and that they may have it more abundantly."

I continued to look at those two bags of seeds and ponder the deeper meaning and application the Lord was trying to communicate to me through them. There were two bags because we have a choice, just as in the garden of Eden. The Lord always gives us a choice. Of course, the first way I saw this applied was to the builder. He was choosing the seeds from the bag provided by the enemy. I saw that by not paying the workers he committed to, he was sowing bad seeds into his business and future. He was only able to look at his current situation and react to not getting paid, and then sow the very seeds that were being sown into him. How many times do we make decisions based on the current situation we face and our reaction to it in the present, not even being able to look to the future or the consequences of those decisions? With our economy in such a challenging state, we, too, are faced every day with trying to look beyond our immediate circumstances with faith and hope, and choosing to sow the seeds of life into our future.

Let me see if I can further explain the application using my own situation. As I face our tenants struggling to pay their rent, I have a choice of what to sow into them and into my own future with each phone call about their current situation. Do I want to sow grace, understanding and hope? Or do I want to sow consequences of eviction, penalties, and no grace or help? I have a choice each time. Our own current financial situation is greatly challenged, so that places additional pressure on my choice of the words that I am sowing. I am choosing to sow grace, life, understanding, and hope to each one, and trusting the Lord to take care of me as well. With the economy the way that it is, the people around us could have a tendency to close up, tighten up, stop helping, and give based on their own situations. When we are in a time of famine is when we need to dig in and press past what we can see, and give whatever we can in faith. Look at the definition of *faith* in Hebrews 11:1: "Now faith is the substance of things hoped for, the evidence of things not seen." So, could we be sowing into what we are hoping for? I think so.

Here is what I, personally, have put into practice for some time now: I sow into what I am hoping for. If I am hoping for encouragement, I sow encouragement into others. If I am hoping for prayer and answers, I sow prayer for others and rejoice in the answers they are getting. Our finances are challenged at the moment, so I am pressing to give when I have the opportunity. When tithing, I am not tithing the exact amount, but challenging myself to round it up. When faced with Christmas presents and tight finances, I signed up to give a present to a needy child, and then purchased a gift a little more expensive than their recommended amount. I purchased blankets for the homeless in Israel, as their winter is cold and there is a need. In a time when the enemy would want me to choose seeds of stinginess, I am trying to sow seeds of giving.

Another interesting event keeps happening that seems related to this very thing. Yesterday, I was purchasing something online as a gift, and I really thought I had it all figured out. Although it was a bit more money than I had intended to spend, I made the purchase, thinking there was really no other choice. Right after I made the purchase, I looked at one other place and found a better deal. I also look at the gas prices; they have dropped so much that two months ago I would never have believed such a sight, and yet, here it is. All this to say that when circumstances, situations, and life seem to look like there is no way out, we can take hope that there is. By taking hold of that hope, we can choose to pick from the seeds of life and sow into our future. Is this not the way the world views our current situation? If you have money, right now you can get great deals on houses and stocks. This is the time to buy, because the increase is coming in the future, maybe not immediately, but it will come; it always has.

The choices that I make today with my words, actions, decisions, giving, and everything else are being sown into my future. If you want a current situation in your life changed, ask the Lord what you can sow now to improve it in the future. To me, this seems like a testimony of the hope that is within us to the people around us who are losing their jobs, homes, finances and everything else (1 Peter 3:15-16).

There are two bags of seeds presented to us each day, one brings life and one brings death. We have a choice. May I encourage you to ponder with the Lord what you can sow, if not money, then encouraging words, a smile, an opening in a long line of traffic. We can sow our time into others too.

The other day, I was taking my son to school, waiting in a long line of traffic to turn. Like always, I asked the Lord for an opening when I got to the front of the line. The Lord asked me why I did not pray for everyone in the line to have a break in the traffic. When I am in a parking lot and looking for a place, I ask the Lord for a good spot, and applying His question to this, I should be asking for the others to find a place, too. In a season of crowds, extra pressures and demands, we have perfect opportunities to look outside of our own selves and sow into others, too. What would the world look like if Christians everywhere started doing this and thinking this way? Is this not the way we are supposed to think? As a thought, have we, as Christians, blended into the world just a little too much?

One more current example in my own life with Wally and his work situation. He went to work for another builder after the one above, and after a week on the job the other workers got paid and all the checks bounced. All the workers decided not to go back to work until they got paid. That morning, Wally and I were talking about the two choices that were before him. He could choose to stay at home and be guaranteed not to get paid, or he could go to work and have the possibility to get paid. Again, the two bags of seeds: one bag is the seeds the world chooses, and the other, the seeds of the kingdom. He chose to go to work, and the owner came by and saw him and another person working, and good seeds were sown. Choosing the bag of good seeds can, at times, go against every part of your flesh. I have come to realize that this is the time you must sow from the bag of good seeds because your future is going to be affected.

IN TIME OF NEED

Three weeks ago today, I walked through a situation that, to my eyes, looked impossible, and I saw God work a miracle. I want to write about it in hopes of encouraging others who also find themselves in situations that look impossible.

Months ago, we had planned to go to California for Christmas to see family, as it had been three years since we had done this. We praise the Lord for airline mileage to make this possible! Wally was driving, while Jordan and I had a flight scheduled to leave on December 19 very early in the morning. The night before we were to leave, I got a phone call from the airline informing me that part of our flight schedule was cancelled because of the weather. I have to tell you, getting this type of call the night before you are scheduled to leave is not fun. For the next three or four hours I was on and off the phone trying to find a way to California through the bad weather. It just so happened that flights for the two days prior had been cancelled as well, and so all of those people were doing the same thing trying to get to their Christmas destinations. This made the rescheduling much more difficult. Finally, at 10:30 the night before, the problem appeared to be settled and the flights scheduled.

When I got up early the next morning, I asked the Lord if I needed to call the airline to verify the flights, and this is what He said. He showed me a picture of a blocker on a football team and a person behind the blocker with the football following through the path that the blocker had made. When I asked the Lord about the picture, He explained to me that He was the blocker and I was the one with the football. I needed to stay behind Him today as He made the way through. I was encouraged and concerned at the same time, as this was a clear indication that the day was going to be a challenge, but at the same time, He had a plan through it. So, we went to the airport.

Everything seemed to be fine as we got on the first flight. The door closed and we headed to the runway, then sat there for about forty-five minutes waiting to take off. We were flying to Chicago, which happened to be in a big snow storm. This forty-five minutes was not a good thing, considering that we only had one hour between our connecting flights. I prayed hard during the flight in between a continuous conversation with the person sitting next to me. The Lord had definitely purposed the seating arrangement, as He gave me words of wisdom that this single father of a fourteen-year-old teenager needed. I was greatly encouraged by the ministry, yet concerned about what the next hours held for Jordan and me to catch our next flight.

When the plane landed, we had fifteen minutes to make our next flight. We went to the shuttle and there was a long line, so I told Jordan we needed to make a run for it. According to the person we asked, it was a fifteen-minute walk to our next gate, so we figured if we ran we could cut it in half. We ran, dodging people and trying with everything we had. This was much easier for my son; Jordan is fourteen and has much more strength then I do.

We got to the gate just as they were pulling the walkway to the plane away. I begged them to please let us on the plane, but they would not. One person after another had done the same thing, but they would not do it, even though the plane sat there for at least ten minutes before moving. We joined the line with the hundreds of other people who had missed their flights.

I remembered the vision and explanation the Lord had given me that morning, and figured this was what He was talking about, so I began to ask Him where He was going. There was another flight to San Francisco that had been delayed, so I was hoping for that. While we were in the line, I decided to call the people I was talking to last night. I stood there looking at all the monitors showing all the departures, and I asked the lady on the phone about all the possible places that were not affected by this snowstorm. As we got to the front of the line, the lady on the phone said that she could get us on another flight that evening, so we got out of line. I sat to the side waiting for her to return on the line with a confirmation and instructions.

As I sat there, I was crying out to the Lord for His direction. *Lord, all I can see is the way before my eyes, but I trust that You have a way out of this that I do not see. Please, Lord, show me the way.* The lady returned on the line and informed me that she was not able to do it. There was absolutely nothing else she could do but refund our tickets. I could not understand how this could help me at all, as we were stranded in Chicago with thousands of others. I kept praying to see where the Lord was blocking. Then, I asked the lady about how it worked to get on standby with a flight. As she explained that I needed to go to the gate, I asked her to help me see something. If we were to somehow get on that flight, was there another flight to Redding? There was one seat on a later flight. I figured if I could get to San Francisco, I could at least rent a car to get to Redding. So Jordan and I walked to the gate to find another very long line. We waited over an hour in the line because no one was at the counter. Finally, someone was at the counter and we got to the front of the line, but they informed us that the standby line was closed, as there were forty- five people already on it and only ten seats available. The lady told me to wait off to the side of the counter. I really felt this was the Lord, so I stayed right there. All the people on the standby list were instructed to go and sit down until their names were called, but we were told to stand right there.

It appeared to be a hopeless situation, but something in me really felt the Lord was going to do something, so we waited. The lady who had told us to stand to the side was the one taking the tickets as the people boarded the plane. Suddenly, within minutes of the plane leaving, the lady told me to get on the plane. She said she needed to fill the seats and get the plane in the air. We boarded the plane, and I sat there, totally amazed at what God had just done. He made a way where there was no way. I could not stop praising the Lord.

Only the Lord could have done what He just did. We were able to get to Chico once we were in San Francisco, and Wally and Amber picked us up. We made it!

I learned something that day that has been life-changing. When we cannot see any way out of our circumstances in life, we truly can depend on the Lord to make a way. I learned to ask the Lord to show me His way, as I really did not see any other options. When I stepped into this place of faith, something within me shifted. For me, it was probably humbling myself before Him and admitting, *Lord, I do not see Your plan. Show me Your plan. I believe You have one.* He does have a plan for each day of our lives; we just have to look for it a little harder sometimes.

Two days ago, I was walking through the book of Romans reading all my highlighted Scriptures, and I came across a Scripture that totally confirmed my airport adventure, "God, who gives life to the dead and calls those things which do not exist as though they did" (Romans 4:17). We did not have tickets for those seats. There were many other people left at the airport that day searching for another flight, and the Lord called forth two seats on that airplane for my son and me to take. I do not plan on ever forgetting what the Lord did for us that day. I have walked a new place of trust with the Lord, and I am ever so grateful for what He has taught me.

I do want to encourage you to position yourself to believe and look for the way through situations that look impossible behind the Lord. He is the blocker, and you are the runner with the ball. The runner just follows the blocker and really cannot see past him; he just stays close and keeps going.

Help us, Lord Jesus! "Let us therefore come boldly to the throne of grace, that we may obtain mercy and find grace to help in time of need" (Hebrews 4:16).

WHAT CONCERNS ME

I love it when a passage of Scripture that I read awakens my spirit to new life! That happened to me with a particular Scripture that I want to share today. On December 27, 2008 during my regular daily reading of the Word, I read Psalm 138:8: "The Lord will perfect that which concerns me; Your mercy, O Lord, endures forever; do not forsake the works of Your hands." When I read, "The Lord will perfect that which concerns me." I became encouraged in my spirit that the Lord was going to take care of what was going on around me.

I have been pondering and standing on that Scripture since then, and have really found this to be true in my life. As I look back through the rearview mirror of the last year or so, I can clearly see the Lord's dealings with my heart in the areas that concerned me, but not in the way that I expected. My mind would think it would mean He would provide a check in the mail when I needed money. My concern is to pay my bills and keep my house, and so money should come to me. Maybe someone will just walk up to me at church and hand me the exact amount of money I need to pay the bill without me even speaking of the need. Or how about the bank calling me and saying that the loan is paid off. Better yet, the bank might say "You have been paying too much, and not only is your loan paid off, but we owe you money!" I think you get the idea; there are lots of ways I think the Lord could perfect that which concerns me. Maybe you do, too. When you look at what the Lord has done for you through the rearview mirror, the things that seemed so big and overwhelming through the front windshield appear amazingly smaller after the Lord has brought you through them.

So, as I look back at my concerns, I can see the Lord doing far more than I ever could have thought or even imagined (Ephesians 3:20). Again, I want to share in hopes of helping others look at their own circumstances and be encouraged that the Lord is doing a good work in them (Philippians 1:6). My first concern, which was no secret, was our finances. I have written many times about this, as I have gone through a long journey of Him perfecting what concerns me. As I look at it today, I see that our financial struggle has compelled me to become wiser in my spending, such as cutting out extra spending and learning to wait for things that in the past I would have just gone and purchased. The examples I will give had multiple effects within me. I had to wait for the haircuts and hair colorings. I can see that this also affected my fear of man and how I look to other people. I can see that it has created within me a new ability to wait.

I am still learning about saving money on groceries by using coupons. Not only am I learning a whole new world of terms and deals, but I am facing my own mindsets about what I thought that was and who did it (the past judgments I have made about others). In the past, I felt good if I saved or used a coupon to save $.50 or $1.00. This last week I saved $26.00 and am encouraged by this savings. This is something that is very new to me, but I really see the value of it in enabling me to be a better steward of what the Lord has given me. I do not believe that I would have pursued this path if our finances had not been a problem. There are much greater savings to be realized, and I am going to learn this, and I am hoping to help others learn too.

I have become a better cook (which is a total miracle), because our situation has compelled me to learn. As you have read in the other writings, God's Word on my concern with finances has affected our views in many areas of life. When He says in His Word that He will perfect that which concerns me, He means things that I do not even know are connected to my limited view of my concerns. He does not just change the bandage, but brings healing to the depths through the circumstances we encounter. This confirms His Word in James 1:2-5 regarding just what the tests and trials are to produce in us and our response of counting it all joy. If we are not counting it all joy yet, we need to ask for His help, and then He will work out Psalm 138:8 deep within us. He goes after it in our mindsets, past judgments, past choices, and everything else that affects that area.

The other areas He is perfecting that have concerned me are being the wife and the mother the Lord created me to be, mostly through me not working outside the home. Last year, the Lord told me not to work. That alone affected just about everything within me with our finances already greatly challenged. Taking it apart further, I can see how that one statement from the Lord exposed pride, fear of man, my self-worth, and my value in contributing to the family finances, as my husband worked so very hard. I can also see that it is producing good in me, too, as a mother to both of my children, physically and spiritually. I am available to them.

I have also learned how to serve my family in taking care of their basic needs. My heart and mind have changed in how I view washing the clothes, doing the dishes, cooking and cleaning. For some, doing these tasks might not be an issue, but for me it was. It exposed the mindsets and resentments that had formed within my heart and made me unable to truly be who the Lord created me to be. These daily duties are becoming my service to our home and my family. I am learning to care for my family, in a whole different way. I also pray for them intensely, and continually ask the Lord to help me. Through the tightening of our finances, the Lord is making me into a woman who cares for her family and is even wiser with money. The years of heart and mind issues are being dealt with too.

I am writing this because I really feel that our season is changing, as finances seem to be opening up, even though in the natural world the economy is getting worse. This reveals that the Lord's hand has truly been on this last year and a half, and that the hard times are lifting. Just this morning we found a cashier's check in our mailbox and we were really blessed. I could write for hours the depth of what the Lord is perfecting in us through this season of what concerns us. I can also see that for months now I have been crying out to the Lord for an understanding heart, wisdom, and a clean heart. He is absolutely answering those prayers, though not in a way that I would have expected, but much, much better. All I have to say is: *Keep going, Lord. I welcome the continuing work of Your hand and ask You not to forsake it. Amen!*

AMAZED AT THE GOOD

I am continually amazed and in awe of how God does things in my life. In the midst of the challenges of life, He somehow finds opportunity within them to enhance who I am in Him. I woke up this morning feeling that Romans 8:28 was actually living and breathing within me. Romans 8:28 reads, "And we know that all things work together for good to those who love God, to those who are the called according to His purpose." My spirit knows this to be true and is awakening to it more and more each day. I will share some of the highlights of the last six to nine months that I have not yet written about, as an encouragement to each reader as they face their own challenges.

The first area that the Lord has been teaching me is the area of judging. I am in no way an expert, but I am learning through the struggles. I felt the Lord started showing me this through the back door, as I had to really focus to see it. During our temporary financial situation, I was noticing certain patterns in my thinking, and I did not know where they were coming from. For example, I received a gift card to Starbucks for Christmas. Starbucks is my favorite place, and this was one of the first areas in which I had to stop spending. I *missed it,* I have to admit, but it revealed an unhealthy attachment I had, so stopping it was good. Needless to say, a gift card for Starbucks was a treasured gift.

Someone paid my way to a conference at our church, so I thought I would stop by Starbucks on the way to get a coffee and sit and enjoy the conference. For me, a coffee is just relaxing. But then the thought came to my mind: *What are people going to think about me having a Starbucks coffee when I have made it pretty clear to some about our financial situation?* I actually found myself wanting to just go get it and enjoy it at home. One time I did go get it and bring it home, but I happened to know the person in the drive-thru and found myself even needing to state that I got the gift card for Christmas. Very silly, I know, but it got my attention, because it seemed quite bizarre. So, I sat with the Lord and asked Him, *What in the world is bringing in these ridiculous thoughts, and why do I believe them and act on them?* He showed me there have been times in my life when I have made judgments against others about similar things, and because I had done this, I opened a back door to the enemy to have access to this against me. I realized that much of the warfare I have encountered is because I passed judgment on others. Some call this stepping out of God's grace. The way to close the door is to repent and ask for forgiveness. I have been on a journey through judgment, looking at circumstances in my past and seeing if I have opened a door to the enemy. This is a true battle of flesh and Spirit, but we are more than conquerors through Him who loved us (Romans 8:37).

Our son, Jordan, fifteen, is learning how to drive. As I sit in the car with him at the wheel, I am pressed to remember how to drive. I have been driving for thirty-one years, and yet, I really have to try to explain how I do it. So many of the things I do are habits, part of how it is done. I turn the car without thinking. I start, stop, park, and drive without thinking much. I have come to realize there are things I have been doing in our marriage that have become habits, and that I really do not want to be doing. I am learning that life and death are in the power of the tongue (Proverbs 18:21). I am realizing that I was made for reproduction, and for creating babies, so within my DNA is the power to create. I have the power within my home to create life or death (Proverbs 14:1). I have new understanding as to why the serpent in the garden went to the woman instead of the man. Paying attention to how I am driving a car has also shown me how I am sowing into my marriage and home. I found myself being critical of nearly everything about my husband of twenty-seven years, and I had to stop it. I had created a habit and it was not good. It had nothing to do with Wally or my love and my commitment to our marriage. It was an issue of my heart that the Lord was highlighting and I was seeing it. I listened to a message of a woman talking about the same issue, and she challenged us to write down ten different good things about our spouse for the next thirty days. I quickly realized that, if you do the math, it would add up to three hundred things. My first response was: *That would be impossible!* That response, in itself, showed me the importance of the task. The first day, I could easily come up with ten things, but the next day I realized I was really going to have to focus on the good in him for the day so that I could find ten new things for the next. This was exactly what it was supposed to do (Philippians 4:8-9). I took it a step further and read the list to my husband, which held me accountable and encouraged him. This started breaking down my pride. I am up to one hundred things, and every couple days, I send the revised list to my husband. He is being encouraged and I am breaking a bad habit. This could be used in every situation where you find yourself being critical of others. Look for the good in them. I really see the sowing and reaping principle at work here.

Through another situation where my husband and I felt really betrayed, I asked the Lord, if I had ever done that to anyone, and, of course, He answered my question that I had. We can take the situations in our lives and find out from the Lord what is really going on and get healing and victory. He is doing this over and over again as Wally is working on the house next door. Although we are tempted, at times, to try to make as much money as we can by him doing all the work himself, the Lord is helping us focus on the needs of others and provide work for them, too. I also became aware of services that we need to have done and pay money for, and to whom we pay the money. I have been burdened to support other Christians I know, if it is possible. For example, in getting our hair cut, I can go to a cheap salon and pay them the money without even knowing the owner or what they stand for, or I can go to a friend of mine and sow into her business of cutting hair. It is a purposed choice. I know there are Christians we know who do not do a very good job, but there are those who need others to sow into them. Through this one job that the Lord gave us, we are seeing ways to sow into the lives of others. *Yeah, God!* The sowing and reaping principle is not just about money, it applies to everything. You need a friend; sow into someone's life. You need encouragement; sow encouragement into someone's life. I think you get the idea.

Through the challenges of life, and in the midst of difficult times in our country, God really can use it to His advantage in our lives. He is teaching me so much. When I look at it now, I do not think I, personally, would have learned these things any other way. I believe this is the *counting it all joy* part of James 1:2 that he is writing about. We are all on our own journey of life with the Lord, so I encourage you in your own journey to *draw near to Him* (James 4:8), and as He draws near, you will be changed. *Yes and Amen!* It really is all about Him, it really is!

I NEED A DAILY UPGRADE

"Be sober (self-controlled), be vigilant (watchful); because your adversary the devil walks about like a roaring lion, seeking whom he may devour" (1 Peter 5:8). Over the past two days, I have had such a practical illustration that I have to share. In the Scripture above, I mainly want to focus on the words *like* and *may*. For nearly two solid days, I have found myself wrestling with my computer. Maybe you, too, have found yourself frustrated with a virus, or it stopped working, or was not doing what you think it should do. What about when it totally shuts off in the middle of something important? Where do those emails go that you sent but were never received? I think they must be hanging out with the socks that seem to not stay connected with their mates when I do the laundry!

The challenge with my computer was that nearly every thirty to sixty seconds, a little window at the bottom right of my screen would pop up, warning me of a virus attacking my computer. Then another larger one would pop up and my computer would slow down considerably. Then my own protecting software would pop up on the other side of my screen, warning me of a virus that I needed to quarantine. I would quarantine it and delete it, and then the cycle would start all over again. If I clicked on the first window that popped up, a spyware program would start scanning my system uninvited. It would tell me all these things it was finding wrong with my computer and asking me if I wanted it to fix it. At first, I clicked the yes button, but the program prompted me to purchase software to fix it. It was like clockwork; as I clicked no over and over, I could see that this spyware was sending the so-called viruses to my computer to get my software to react, and then wear me down so much that I would buy the product just to make it go away.

I have to tell you, I was getting so annoyed with it. I was determined not to pay the money, and I was angry that it had access. I finally was divinely inspired to realize that there was a cookie deposited into my computer from this company, which gave them total access as long as I was on the Internet. I deleted the cookie, restarted my computer, and it was all gone, and has been gone ever since. *Praise God!*

Why in the world am I writing about this? I saw how this spyware company was like the devil, acting like it was a roaring lion, wanting me to believe something was wrong with my computer and that I was going to lose everything if I did not purchase their product. I saw that as the devil continually walking around like something he is not. The devil wants to annoy, frustrate, steal, distract, wear down and try to convince me to come into agreement with him (purchase the product) to bring peace in a situation. This spyware (interesting name that implies deception and going places undetected) kept bothering me, just like the enemy does. When I recognized the access point and closed that door, then it went away. We have access points where we have given into compromise, cheating, and anywhere we have fallen to the "cookie/temptation" he set before us. Look at the Word in Ephesians 4:26-27: "Be angry, and do not sin: do not let the sun go down on your wrath, nor give place to the devil." There is a "cookie," my friends, right there. The Lord is exposing a place where we can potentially give place to or create an opening for the devil to have access. When he has access, he is out for blood. He is out to steal, kill, and destroy as in John 10:10.

When we recognize where we have given that place (update in the Word and time with the Lord), then we repent and the access is closed. The cookies are deleted. The beginning of the Scripture above starts out with us being sober and vigilant. Could this also be instructing us in what we choose to do today with what is coming against us? Could this apply to what we think, say, how we react and respond to people and situations on our path today? Could the situations that are frustrating us today be exposing "cookies/access points" from the past that we can close and have victory? I think so!

A Scripture that reinforces this would be 2 Corinthians 10:3-6: "For though we walk in the flesh, we do not war according to the flesh. For the weapons of our warfare are not carnal but mighty in God for pulling down strongholds, casting down arguments and every high thing that exalts itself against the knowledge of God, bringing every thought into captivity to the obedience of Christ, and being ready to punish all disobedience when your obedience is fulfilled."

Strongholds are mindsets that we have allowed to be built in our minds, usually as reactions to hurts, failures, disappointments, lies and many other things that the enemy does to get us not to see the truth. The spyware was trying to convince me something was wrong with my computer, when it was not. The enemy sets up arguments within our minds about right and wrong, fair and not fair, to set within our minds things that will exalt themselves against the knowledge of God, which brings His truth in a situation. This would be a really good reason to get the Word of God continuously into our hearts and minds. We need daily updates, revisions and insight into the schemes of the enemy. When we choose to remain angry in a situation, we give the devil an access point to then infiltrate all of our thinking. The devil is a virus to our minds. He sends thoughts to try to infect us. If we are not sober and vigilant all the time, then we will have additional battles to fight in the days ahead, just like I watched my software continually combat the lies . It comes down to a daily choice to be influenced by the words, ways and things of God, or by the world's thoughts and ways.

It is a fight, a purposed, focused, and diligent fight of faith every day. The weapons of our warfare are not earthly, but mighty in God to expose all the "cookies" that the enemy has placed in our minds, and we can be more than conquerors through Christ Jesus (Romans 8:37). We can do all things through Christ who strengthens us (Philippians 4:13). Everything is through Jesus Christ, not in our own power. We will lose the battle over and over again doing this in our own strength. Walking in the flesh is death; walking in the Spirit is life (Romans 8:1-8).

I hope this has uncovered the lies of the enemy by exposing his schemes and opening up God's truth in the situation. I pray that peace will rule (Philippians 4:8-9). I hope that the relevance and life-application value of the Word lights up truths within you in your situations as well. Are the pop-ups obvious or subtle? I close with Psalm 119:105: "Your word is a lamp to my feet and a light to my path." *Thank You, Jesus!*

HE WILL BE THERE

The other day, I was driving to the airport to pick up Amber, and the Lord dropped a revelation into my spirit about faith. Amber is in an airplane, believing that I am going to pick her up at the airport. She cannot see me or talk to me (cell phones off while flying). She has to stay on the plane and believe that if I said I was going to be there to pick her up, I will be. I saw this to be exactly what faith is. Through the challenges we encounter in life, there are many times when we cannot see what the Lord is doing on our behalf to help, provide for, and bring about for us, but we can believe that He is there for us by faith. We can take Him at His Word that says, "If you can believe, all things are possible to him who believes" (Mark 9:23). "Yet in all these things we are more than conquerors through Him who loved us" (Romans 8:37). "And we know that all things work together for good to those who love God, to those who are the called according to His purpose" (Romans 8:28). It takes focusing on Jesus; who He is, His faithfulness to us in the past, and holding on to His Word that gets us through situations. We cannot see Him doing anything at times, but we have to choose to trust and believe each day that He is, just as Amber had to believe that I was going to be there at the airport to pick her up.

Amber did not really have to worry too much about me being *there,* even though she could not see me driving, or see me at the *airport* until she came down the escalator. Because of years of me *doing* what I said I would do, she knew that I was going to be there. We also had many hours of phone conversations prior to her trip. She knew very clearly that I knew her schedule and what time she was going to get in. I told her I would be there and she believed me. Could this be what the situations in our lives are working into us as we choose each day to believe and trust that He is going to take care of us, and when we experience situations that stretch beyond our brain capacity to reason the solution? Yes, it is! We can be encouraged today that the Lord is working where we cannot see Him working.

I also look at the relationship that Amber and I have established through the years of her life. As her mother, I have nurtured, prayed for, and been there for her in the good and bad times. Yes, there are times that I have not responded as I should have, being an earthly, carnal parent. This is not how God the Father responds to us. We develop our relationship with Him through spending time with Him, worshipping Him, focusing on Him, and allowing His Word to direct our paths each moment. Just as Amber and I have developed a relationship together learning to trust each other, this parallels our walk with the Lord. We can trust that He will be at the airport to pick us up, even though we cannot see Him driving there, or see what He is doing on our behalf ahead of us.

Even thinking of Amber's view from the airplane, I can see that if it were possible, she could see far clearer the path I have to take to the airport as she would have a different perspective than I do. My perspective from the ground is limited. The Lord has a much better perspective of our circumstances.

Encouragement from His Word:

— "Now, faith is the substance of things hoped for, the evidence of things not seen" (Hebrews 11:1).

— "Jesus Christ is the same yesterday, today, and forever" (Hebrews 13:8). Thank You, Jesus!

— "For we walk by faith, not by sight" (2 Corinthians 5:7).

— "Let us draw near with a true heart in full assurance of faith, having our hearts sprinkled from an evil conscience and our bodies washed with pure water. Let us hold fast the confession of our hope without wavering, for He who promised is faithful. And let us consider one another in order to stir up love and good works" (Hebrews 10:22-24).

Today, may you find your faith in the Lord Jesus Christ expanded and strengthened through your circumstances. May you just find Him closer and closer through it all. He knew you before you were born (Psalm 139) and He knows what you are made of because He put it there. He has a plan and purpose for you in each day (Jeremiah 29:11-13). *Thank You, Jesus!*

BY FAITH, BY FAITH

Over the last few weeks, I have been made aware of something over and over again, and have positioned my thoughts to meditate on what the Holy Spirit is showing me. Today, I want to write about something that is once again changing the way I think, speak, respond and react in daily situations.

For a very long time, I have been intrigued about the great cloud of witnesses that surround us, in Hebrews 12:1: "Therefore we also, since we are surrounded by so great a cloud of witnesses, let us lay aside every weight, and the sin which so easily ensnares us, and let us run with endurance the race that is set before us." For me, the focus has been on the phrase, "Therefore we also." To me, this indicates that it is connecting chapter 12 with the previous chapter 11, which is about the "hall of faith." I see these men and women of the past as the great cloud of witnesses. The Lord shows us who these witnesses are that are cheering for us.

I see this stadium at night, of course, with all the bright lights on and much cheering and shouting. I see each of us approaching the tunnels that lead to the field, and as we enter, we are being cheered for and encouraged to keep going on our race. I love this picture, and it encourages me very much.

I have equally been made aware of 2 Corinthians 11:14-15: "And no wonder! For satan himself transforms himself into an angel of light. Therefore it is no great thing if his ministers also transform themselves into ministers of righteousness, whose end will be according to their works." The Holy Spirit has connected these two passages of Scripture for me. The enemy imitates the ways of heaven just enough to try to trick us or trip us up. Remember, "the thief (satan) does not come except to steal, and to kill, and to destroy. I (Jesus) have come that they may have life, and that they may have it more abundantly" (John 10:10). The enemy even tried his tricks on Jesus when He walked the earth, but Jesus was wise and did not fall for them. He is our example (1 Peter 2:21-25). So what does all this mean to us today?

May I suggest that, since there is a great cloud of witnesses surrounding us in the third heaven (2 Corinthians 12:1-5), the enemy, too, would have a cloud of witnesses in the second heaven? The second heaven is the realm of the enemy (Daniel 10:12-13). I have noticed that we are continually encountering these two groups, and we have a choice by what we say as to which group we engage. I recently was in a situation in which I was made aware of this. A person walked into the room and asked a question, and my response determined the outcome of the rest of the evening. If I had chosen to be critical, then the second heaven would have gladly joined in, but instead, I stepped right over it and did not bite the poison apple. In days past, I would have, but not this time. I have noticed that I am fighting choices I made in the past. When I have chosen to participate in talking about something in the wrong way, it seemed to feed something within me. The more I fed this negative thing, the more it became a way of life. The enemy is always waiting for us to speak just one negative word, as that empowers him. Can you see it? When we are with a group of people, we have two realms cheering us on? We have a choice continually before us to choose life or death with our words (Proverbs 18:21). Whether it is talking about a person, situation, organization or anything else we have two groups around us wanting to engage with us and contribute to the conversation. I believe the "Hall of Faith" people in chapter 11 is the group that I want to choose to join with.

How can we change conversations to be filled with life? How can we be continually aware of these two groups of witnesses wanting to influence us? We can pray for the wisdom in James 1:5. We can ask for the eyes of our understanding to be enlightened in Ephesians 1:18-19. We can approach every situation looking for the good in it, because, realistically, if God causes all things to work together for the good, as in Romans 8:28, then there is good mixed in with all the other stuff. If we focus on the good, we will see it. We will see the words of life that are in us begin to speak into the situations of others.

His Word is filled with help, encouragement and life. His Word of truth continually supports and builds upon itself. The verses all work together to see us through every moment of every day we are given. *Oh Holy Spirit, please help us to stay connected to the third heaven at all times. Open the eyes of our understanding to see all the "By faith" verses, as the people we are walking by, cheering us on, and that one day we get to join with to cheer for others who come after us.* By faith these people are cheering us on and we can run the race with endurance. *Yeah, God!*

LEARNING TO BE CONTENT

For some time now, I have been examining something that the Apostle Paul wrote in Philippians, and I wanted to share it as I continue to wonder and dig for the hidden treasures of Paul's journeys of life. After all, in Philippians 4:9, he wrote, "The things which you learned and received and heard and saw in me, these do, and the God of peace will be with you.'" I want the God of peace to be with me, and I want to understand what Paul was talking about particularly in Philippians 4:11-13: "Not that I speak in regard to need, for I have learned in whatever state I am, to be content: I know how to be abased, and I know how to abound. Everywhere and in all things I have learned both to be full and to be hungry, both to abound and to suffer need. I can do all things through Christ who strengthens me."

I have been intrigued with the words *learned to be content*. This would indicate to me that being content is something we grow into and takes time. It does not appear that we ask for it, but that we learn it. In James, we see that we can ask for wisdom (James 1:5) if we feel we lack it. But Paul wrote that he had learned to be content, which means being satisfied. Paul learned to be satisfied in whatever state, situation or circumstance he found himself in, which tells me that this is for all of us.

What does the word *content* mean to you? Think about it. As I thought about it, I found that content could be thought of as doing nothing. I could think about my current situation and think I am to be content and so not pursue any kind of change. I do not need to fight my circumstances but just accept them. Desire nothing and just be where I am. What I found as I tried to be content in every situation, was that I was continually frustrated, and, at times, discouraged as I tried to walk out the prophetic words that have been spoken over me, or the dreams that I have for my life. So, the following is what I have discovered about learning to be content.

I looked up 2 Corinthians 1:8-11, 4:7-10, and 11:22-28, which described some of the intense struggles and trying situations that Paul encountered. When I looked at my thoughts on being content, and Paul's circumstances that helped him learn to be content, I saw that he did anything but just stay still. The more he did, the greater the challenges he encountered. I wonder how many times I have stopped short of where I was going because I ran into opposition, and thought I must be doing the wrong thing because it was hard. Good thing Paul did not think that way, or we would not have very much written down from him. I will continue, but feel free to camp here for a bit if you need to, because that thought in itself is worth pondering.

Then I wanted to look at what he learned and wrote about in 2 Corinthians 3:5, 9:6-10, 4:11-18, and 1 Timothy 6:6-10. (I am not writing all of these out, but take a look at some of these, especially if you need to be encouraged about your own situation.) I found it all summed up in these verses in Philippians 4:6-8: "Be anxious for nothing, but in everything by prayer and supplication, with thanksgiving, let your requests be made known to God; and the peace of God, which surpasses all understanding; will guard your hearts and minds through Christ Jesus. Finally, brethren, whatever things are true, whatever things are noble, whatever things are just, whatever things are pure, whatever things are lovely, whatever things are of good report, if there is any virtue and if there is anything praiseworthy — meditate on these things." This is how he did it through all of the challenges and struggles.

For some reason, I found that I need a bit more help to focus on being content in every circumstance I encounter. This is what I have gleaned from it. I am choosing to look at my circumstances as opportunities to find God in them by seeking Him for wisdom and answers, receiving peace, learning to focus on the Lord and find out who He is in me. This will help establish additional history with the Lord for future circumstances, and gain new and refreshed understanding of the fact that I can do all things through Christ who strengthens me (Philippians 4:13). I can be encouraged that I have opportunities to grow in faith and my trust in the Father, Son, and Holy Spirit. We need to grow in wisdom, assurance and patience, and when we do, the very things we ask from the Lord may come as answers to the situations we are in.

What we learn is to look beyond the present, knowing it is temporary, and walk in confidence that Jesus has a good plan. Learning to be content is a daily positioning of ourselves not to be tossed about by our circumstances. I believe that Jesus was modeling this when He was asleep in the boat during the storm. Every challenge is an opportunity for us to grow closer to Jesus. We are learning to be content, as Paul learned, not by just sitting and doing nothing in our circumstances, but by getting back up and choosing to believe, trust, and by finding God through the situation. I close with the words that Jesus spoke to His disciples in Mark 10:27: "With men it is impossible, but not with God; for with God all things are possible." Be encouraged that you are growing in Jesus through it all. *Amen!*

OVERCOME BY TESTIMONIES

L ately, I have been thinking about the power of the testimony. The Lord has been urging me to see something new and life-changing about a testimony.

Revelation 12:10-11: "Then I heard a loud voice saying in heaven, 'Now salvation, and strength, and the kingdom of our God, and the power of His Christ have come, for the accuser of our brethren, who accused them before our God day and night, has been cast down. And they overcame him by the blood of the Lamb and by the word of their testimony, and they did not love their lives to the death.'" What if this is written about you and me? What if the words "they overcame him by the blood of the Lamb and by the word of their testimony" are a key given to us for a greater place of freedom? My friends, the entire Bible is the testimony of Jesus. It empowers us every time we open it and allow it to work within us. I love testimonies. I am encouraged and feel so much better after hearing them. Could it be that something is released into the spiritual realm when speaking of the goodness and faithfulness of God? Absolutely! I think that is why we are encouraged to keep going.

Let us look further into the Word for more that He has to reveal to us. In Deuteronomy 8:2: "And you shall remember that the Lord your God." Verse 18: "And you shall remember the Lord your God," and verse 19: "Then it shall be, if you by any means forget the Lord your God, and follow other gods, and serve them and worship them, I testify against you this day that you shall surely perish." We are instructed to remember what the Lord our God has done for us. Why? It is because that is one of the ways He empowers us to keep walking the path He has called us on.

This is how we face walls, obstacles, hindrances and everything else that comes against us. Let us journey to a time in David's life when he faced the giant Goliath. As I read 1 Samuel 17, I was particularly drawn to verse 36 which was David's testimony, "Your servant has killed both lion and bear; and this uncircumcised Philistine will be like one of them, seeing he has defied the armies of the living God." Who was David testifying to? He was testifying to himself because everyone around him was hiding and scared. I believe he was speaking out the power of the testimony for himself so that he could walk in the strength and courage of it. He was strengthening himself, which means that we can do the same thing. Then, I read verse 39: "David fastened his sword to his armor and tried to walk, for he had not tested them. And David said to Saul, 'I cannot walk with these, for I have not tested them.'"

David did not have a testimony of victory with the armor, but he had strength and courage in his testimony as he remembered what God did for him. He, again, reminds himself just before throwing the fatal stone in verses 45-48, with more testimony building his courage, and then it is over in verse 49. This is a testimony for us! This is how we face the giants in our lives; we remember what God has done for us and speak them ahead of where we are going.

As a caution, the testimony of someone else in a similar situation does not mean that you will get the exact result they did, but you can grab hold of faith and their victory to empower yours.

We see in the Old Testament where people built altars as reminders of important events where God did something, like the stones at the crossing of the river Jordan (Joshua 4). Just as a side note, one of the meanings of *testament* is "any proof that serves as evidence of something." The meaning of *testimony* is "a declaration or affirmation of fact or truth." We have an Old Testament and a New Testament, which teaches and empowers us. Everything within those pages is available to us. Looking at the New Testament, we can also see that as in John 4:39: "And many of the Samaritans of that city believed in Him because of the word of the woman who testified, 'He told me all that I ever did.' " Our testimony has the empowerment to bring others to Him.

The Bible is one of the most amazing gifts that the Father could have given us to help us in our daily lives. It is testimony that still brings life. It is testimony that releases the possibility of God into our situations. When we hear a testimony, we are encouraged and empowered because the POSSIBLE of God (Mark 10:27) is released into the realm in which we are living. We have an opportunity to grab it and turn our impossibilities into possibilities. When we hear a testimony of a healing and we need that healing, too, or someone we know needs it, we can grab it. When we hear prophetic words that may apply to a situation we are facing, those words are released in the physical and in the spiritual realm, and we can embrace them for ourselves.

The testimony of the God of the impossibilities we face in life releases His power to bring what seems to be impossible into the realm of possibility for us. This is why we can do all things through Christ who strengthens us (Philippians 4:13). This is why we are more than conquerors through Him who loved us (Romans 8:37). The very Book that we can read and study every day we live here on earth, has the potential to empower us through everything. We just have to open it up.

I will end with Revelation 12:10-11: "Then I heard a loud voice saying in heaven, 'Now salvation, and strength, and the kingdom of our God, and the power of His Christ have come, for the accuser of our brethren, who accused them before our God day and night, has been cast down. And they overcame him by the blood of the Lamb and by the word of their testimony, and they did not love their lives to the death.'"

Be encouraged this day. If your current situation looks a bit over whelming or impossible (like Goliath), then may I encourage you to remember what God has brought you through, and praise Him; testifying in front of your Goliath just like David did. This will empower you to defeat whatever is trying so hard to stop you. *To God be the glory, GREAT things He has done and will continue to do.* "JESUS CHRIST IS THE SAME YESTERDAY, TODAY, AND FOREVER" (Hebrews 13:8).

It is so important to give your testimony whenever you can. As a result, others can come to know Jesus for themselves, or other believers can be encouraged to continue in the faith. *Amen!* May you remember what He has brought you through so faith will rise up within you!

A VISION WITH POWER

Over the past several months, I have been seeing a vision over and over again. I feel like I am living within this vision and continuously ponder its meaning. This morning, more of it has opened up, so I want to write about it.

Here is the vision: *I see a homeless person on the outside of an eating establishment looking through the window at the people and families inside enjoying fellowship and the food placed before them. I feel the pain of the homeless person as he hungers physically and emotionally, and remembers when he was on the other side of the glass enjoying life. Now he finds himself only with the memories and pain with no doorway to get to the other side.*

I have been dwelling on this vision every day for at least three months, I see myself as the homeless person. I see myself with the memories of the past, with a successful business, dream home, many friends, and the finances to buy everything that I wanted. I see myself looking at others who are successful and have good-paying jobs, and wonder what that would feel like again. At the moment, it feels as if everything we try to start seems to go nowhere. I remember the days when we could always make money, but today we find ourselves with only the memories. In fact, my husband finds jobs and works very hard for the people, only to find himself in situations where he does not get paid at all, or the rules change as the job goes on. What was thought to be agreed upon for pay changes with the wind. We started a business that found no sales from October until now. We can blame it all on the economy, and that might partially be true, but I believe the real truth is that the Lord is working on us. We press our faces on the glass of that restaurant and remember when we could freely go out to dinner and not be concerned about how to pay for it. I really am not feeling sorry for myself, just catching you up on this part of our journey.

Right now, I feel as though I am the person in the vision who is on the outside looking in. I thought about what I did when I was a person on the inside looking out and seeing the person looking in. Did I help them? I believe I did. This "looking in" definitely brings a new perspective on life. What do I do with the questions from family and others who are looking back at me through the window? What do I do with my own feelings of looking through the window? I need to hand it to Jesus, the author and finisher of my faith, and trust Him with each situation as it presents itself.

This morning, I have seen this vision as a mindset of a life based on the ways of the world and what is important to man; a perception of what I think it is like on the other side in people's lives. What I think a spiritual walk with the Lord is to look, feel and be like. Is this from teachings? Is this from what I have heard, watched at the movies or seen on television? I think it is all of the above.

I am beginning to see this vision as a place where my mind is being transformed and renewed like in Romans 12:2: "And do not be conformed to this world, but be transformed by the renewing of your mind, that you may prove what is that good and acceptable and perfect will of God." He is exposing all the places in my mind that have been conformed to this world, and is giving me the opportunity to see them and submit them to Him. On the inside of me, I am actually excited through this time of testing, I can see He is working. He is answering the prayers of my heart for more of Him.

He is answering the prayers of my heart for His thoughts and not mine. I see Him taking me to a place where I see my past and all the memories and thoughts associated with it, yet I am unable to be there and keep looking in that direction because that is all I have been able to see. Maybe He just wants me to let go, turn, and start walking a new way. Maybe, as we let go of absolutely everything and trust Him, He will begin to provide in ways that we have never seen or even heard of. I thought I had done this three and half years ago, but this feels much deeper, and so I say yes to His plans and purposes for this season. I say yes to Him.

I have come to realize that when we hear the testimonies of other's victories, we have the potential to allow perceptions to be set up in our minds that they just asked God to do this and He did it. *Wow, that was awesome, but what about me, Lord? What about the day-in and day-out challenge to believe that You will do that for me? Have we not heard their battle to the victory?* Do we just listen to the challenge and miss the journey and focus on the ending? How do we process all the messages we hear, or His Word as we read it? Do we even recognize when we hit that glass, or do we just break it? We can find Scriptures to justify that action (Matthew 11:12), but is that His way?

I do not have all the answers, but I do know this: He who has begun a good work in me will complete it and work on it until the day of Jesus Christ (Philippians 1:6). I do know that the more I purpose in my mind to meditate on whatever things are true, whatever things are noble, whatever things are just, whatever things are pure, whatever things are lovely, whatever things are of good report, if there is any virtue, and if there is anything praiseworthy—meditate on these things (Philippians 4:8), I find His peace in the storms, and I know that I can count it all joy as I go through various trials (James 1:2). This is because I know, feel and see that it is producing a new mindset, faith, growth and healing. I am learning to meditate on His Word to find the answers in this daily life of faith.

Everything is being shaken on the earth right now, which releases fear. Because of this I am actively releasing His love over my life and family and on the earth. What does His love look like that casts out all this fear (1 John 4:18)? Look at 1 Corinthians 13:4-8 and meditate on that. Before I can give that love, I must have it. It is a daily, moment-by-moment journey for all of us. My prayer is that all will embrace this present season and allow it to expose and work in us. Then we will walk in 1 Peter 3:15: "But sanctify the Lord God in your hearts, and always be ready to give a defense to everyone who asks you a reason for the hope that is in you, with meekness and fear."

Lord, may it be on earth as it is in heaven! Blessings in overflowing capacity to you and your family in these days. We are a blessed people. *Thank You, Jesus! Amen!*

"But whoever keeps His word, truly the love of God is perfected in him. By this we know that we are in Him" (1 John 2:5).

A WORKING TESTIMONY

Selling two houses and shutting everything down to move across the United States is a bit trying at times. I know that God is going to get us through, and we will look back and see that our faith has grown. We will have a powerful testimony of obeying the voice of God and surrendering our lives to follow Him, but the days that lead up to that testimony seem to be filled with many tests.

As I look into the Word, I am reminded of the woman in Mark 5:25-34 who had a flow of blood for twelve years. We do not even get her name. She had been to many doctors and suffered many things from them. She had spent all the money she had and was no better but actually got worse. She was an outcast; she had an incurable sickness, had no money and had been set apart for twelve years. Women flowing with blood were considered unclean (Leviticus 15:19). Though she did not realize it, this woman was working on her testimony! In verse 27 everything changed. When she heard about Jesus, she came behind Him and touched Him and was made well. He spoke to her and proclaimed that she was well (physical healing), acknowledged her (emotional healing), and then told her that her faith had made her well (spiritual healing). Wow, what a testimony she had!

In Mark 10:46-52, we find blind Bartimaeus who sat by the side of the road begging. He was also working on his testimony and did not know it. Day after day, this blind beggar would hear the people walking by telling the miracles of Jesus. Because of his response when he met Jesus, I am surmising that he sat there wondering about what it would be like to meet such a man and to be able to see him. He was working on his testimony. He met Jesus and asked for his sight, and Jesus gave it to him. He did not ask Him for money, He asked for what he had heard and dreamed of that Jesus could do for him. He had his testimony.

I have thought a lot about the story of the man at the Pool of Bethesda in John 5:5-9, and how he had an infirmity thirty-eight years. He waited day after day for his chance to be healed, but someone always stepped down in front of him when the water was stirred. It would appear he felt life was unfair and hopeless. I am assuming this because of his response to Jesus' question, "Do you want to be made well?" He does not answer the question but starts giving his reasons for why it has not happened. His answer was standing right in front of him, and he could not recognize it. Why? It was because he was focusing on what was not happening instead of focusing on what could be happening. That did not stop Jesus; He healed him anyway. Even when the man was asked who healed him, he could not tell them until later. He had a testimony and did not even know it.

There are many stories of real people's lives recorded in the Word to encourage those of us working on our own testimonies. We all have times when we need to continue to believe in God even when it would appear to the natural eye that nothing is happening. Some days the battle to believe is harder than it is other days, but those are opportunities to grow. Maybe you need a job, money to pay your bills. Maybe you need a buyer for your house, a child is not following the Lord, or perhaps you have a family problem. Whatever it may be, know that you are working on and walking out your testimony. Get the most out of it. Choose to trust and focus on Him. I find that if I focus too much on the end result, I miss the joy of the journey.

Your situation is not too big for God to handle, and if it appears He is not handling it, it might be because the journey is teaching you something. Enjoy!

490 TIMES OF FORGIVENESS

"Then Peter came to Him and said, 'Lord, how often shall my brother sin against me, and I forgive him? Up to seven times?' Jesus said to him, 'I do not say to you, up to seven times, but up to seventy times seven' " (Matthew 18:21-22). Most likely, Peter had someone sinning against him, and he was looking for how many times he had to keep forgiving the person who was doing this. He probably felt that seven times was plenty, maybe even the number of times he had forgiven the person. Why the question? Was he asking because he was looking for the number of times he had to make the right decision and then he would have permission to get even? How about call down fire from heaven? The disciples had asked for that. Ever felt like that?

Forgiveness is challenging to walk in. Jesus tells us to forgive seventy times seven; that is 490 times! Peter could have asked one more question for us: Is that per day? I feel like I am on a treadmill of forgiving. By now I should have a career in it. No matter how many times I face situations where I have to forgive, I seem not to see the situation coming until it is in my face. Helping, ministering to, encouraging, loving, and being there for people is wonderful, but sometimes working with people creates a challenge (just being real).

When we get hurt by what someone does or says, what has a tendency to rise up at first is to think, "How dare they?" "What were they thinking? " That is not fair, they have no right to do that, why can they not see they are wrong!" " That was not nice." Another response is to get upset and try to get back at them. Does any of this sound familiar? Just this week, I was tested on this again, and I took a deep breath and asked the Lord for His help. As badly as my flesh wanted to focus on it, I knew that was very dangerous. I asked the Lord to help me forgive.

Then, I had a revelation that greatly helped me. I sat with the Lord and spoke this: *Lord, You are a just God and You know my thoughts and motives in all of this, and You know their motives equally well. You are my Father and You have good plans for me, You are for me and You care about this situation. I believe that You know best in this situation, and whether I ever see them walk through the consequences of what they have sown just now or not, I trust You.* I really focused on this and aligned myself with the mind of Christ. Forgiving someone does not mean that what they did was right; it just means that you are choosing Jesus instead of the enemy, who is out to steal, kill and destroy. It is so much better for your future to choose forgiveness. *Help us all, Jesus, as sometimes we are the one who others need to forgive, and help us not to be blinded to that fact.*

The parable Jesus tells after this conversation is an alternate explanation of forgiveness to Peter, in terms all of us can understand. He talks about a certain king forgiving a servant, and then that servant going out and not forgiving those who owed him, and then the king finding out and throwing that person in jail. I think Jesus is telling Peter He is that certain king. Jesus died on the cross for our sins; and when one of His children hurts us, we do not always want to choose to forgive, just as the servant above. We can sometimes forget what Jesus did for us, the amount that He forgave us, and withhold forgiveness from others.

We know that this parable is relevant to us because of verse 35: "So my heavenly Father also will do to you if each of you, from his heart, does not forgive his brother his trespasses" (Matthew 18:35). Forgiving others frees us. At the time, it is a challenge, but ultimately is very freeing!

Final Note from the Author

I hope you have been enriched, challenged, and encouraged and have seen the hand of Jesus within the pages you have read.

If for some reason you have received this book and you do not know Jesus as your personal Savior, I want you to know that you can. Just repeat this simple prayer to begin your amazing journey with Jesus.

Dear Jesus,

Thank You for loving me and for dying on the cross for me. I ask that You please forgive me of my sins and that You come into my heart. I need You and want to get to know You. Show me who You are. I want to love You. In Jesus' name. Amen.

It is that simple. Welcome to the family of God! May I encourage you to please get connected with a local church family that will help you learn more about what you have just done. If you do not know of one, please contact me and I will help you find one.

About the Author

Cheryl Stasinowsky is a speaker and writer of passion and transparency. Her desire is for others to see Jesus in everything they walk through; growing a new passion for His Word and its relevance for them. Please contact her to make arrangements for your future events, retreats, church services, meetings, and conferences. She would love to meet you!

www.hishiddentreasure.blogspot.com

psalm421@surewest.net

Connect with Cheryl on Facebook and twitter @histreasures too!

What others are saying:

Cheryl Stasinowsky is a treasure. Cheryl is a special artist that paints her teachings in faith constructionism, and as such, she passionately extracts the blueprints from the foundation of the Word and then builds that foundation into the details of everyday practical life. Her books and teachings are a life guide, and her speaking appearances are personal. She opens herself to each person she is teaching, and lays out in honesty her own personal experiences of the presence of God within the joys and pains of everyday life."

More Titles by Cheryl Stasinowsky

Deeper Relevance
ISBN: 978-0-6159069-9-7

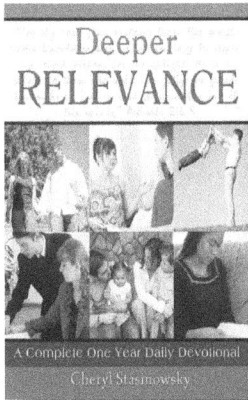

Cheryl set out to write a daily encouraging word on her social networks, not realizing that her pursuit for a deeper understanding of God's Word would blossom into a full devotional. Grab your Bible, along with this book, and get ready to discover kingdom nuggets that will enrich your walk and relationship with Jesus. His Word truly sustains us every day!

Private Moments With God
ISBN: 978-0-6159103-7-6

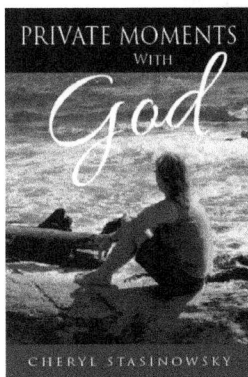

Life as we individually know it ... Each of us has a past that is influencing how we see our present. We walk through our day with all of the pressures and demands of life with a past, in the present, and also with a hope for a future. I, too, journey this thing called life. Through it all, I have come to value to the highest degree the first moments of my early mornings when the house is quiet, it is still dark outside, my coffee is freshly brewed, my iPod is playing worship music in my ears, and I open the Word of God for my nourishment and encouragement for the day. These are those moments ...

More Titles by Cheryl Stasinowsky

Now Faith
ISBN: 978-0-615899-07-7

Now Faith is a face-to-face encounter with the men and women of Hebrews 11 who had the kind of faith that pleased God and moved mountains. Each chapter steps inside their lives, takes a look around, finds vital parts of the DNA of their faith, and then supplies a prayer for the impartation of that faith.

Now Faith is also available in Spanish

Es Pues La Fe
ISBN: 978-0-615899-67-1

All of Cheryl's books can be found on Amazon and most online book sources.
Her books are also available as e-books.

www.ingramcontent.com/pod-product-compliance
Lightning Source LLC
LaVergne TN
LVHW051520080426
835509LV00017B/2127